COUNTEE CULLEN

AND THE NEGRO RENAISSANCE

was not surprised that after a day and a night in the Brooks home he was sent out to fend for himself.

Building a mission into a church was a challenge that Dr. Cullen accepted with fierce enthusiasm. Sometimes he did not have enough money to eat properly, but he was a persistent worker and gradually he built a good-sized membership. As yet he had not thought of marriage because he was investing all the money he could spare to build a small house in Fairmount so that his mother could enjoy a few comforts and conveniences in her old age. But she died after he had been only a few years in New York. He then turned his thoughts to the selection of a wife. He talked this problem over with the Lord, who sent him an answer in a dream where he saw a picture of the woman he would marry.

Soon thereafter he went to Atlantic City for a brief vacation. While he was there the Asbury Methodist Church scheduled a musical concert. Frederick settled his lean frame into a rather uncomfortable seat and prepared to endure the usually screechy soprano, the off-key basso, and the unharmonious chorus. Then suddenly the voice of an angel wakened him from his apathy. He looked at the platform and there she stood, the very woman he had seen in his dream. She had the same pompadour of red-brown hair, the tall well-proportioned figure, the printed challis dress, and the glorious singing voice. Right then and there Frederick Cullen fell in love with Carolyn Belle Mitchell.

A fellow minister introduced them. Cullen lost no time in expressing his interest, but Miss Mitchell reminded

8

worries. Then, too, his mother could not help him; she herself was in need. Sometimes Fred's ambition seemed impossible, but with the help of the Lord and a summer job as a waiter, he got his theological degree.

After two years of pastoring in small towns in Maryland, Cullen received his assignment to Salem in the Harlem section of New York City. At that time it was only a mission of St. Mark's Methodist Episcopal Church. St. Mark's, then located downtown on West Fifty-third Street, was one of the largest Negro churches in town. The pastor, Dr. William H. Brooks, was concerned about the spiritual welfare of the colored people who were now beginning to move to Harlem in large numbers. So he had started a mission in a small storeroom on St. Nicholas Avenue near 124th Street, and when Frederick Cullen was sent to assist him, he assigned the young man to take over the new work.

Cullen soon learned that Dr. Brooks intended him to stand on his own feet. The older man was reserved and soft-spoken. He stood tall and erect, his dark skin clear and scrubbed. His pince-nez glasses with a black silk cord hanging from one lens gave him a scholarly appearance. And indeed he was a studious man. A graduate of Howard University, he had later studied in England, Germany, and France. Early in the mornings he arose to review his foreign languages before starting to prepare for his ministerial work. He delivered his academic sermons quietly and conducted the Sunday services in strict accordance with Methodist Episcopal ritual. Frederick Cullen could tell that this man had high standards of efficiency. So he

Soon after, Frederick Cullen went home to Fairmount to teach. For two years he struggled with Negro country boys and girls who were desperately eager to learn to read and write and figure. Unfortunately they were ill-equipped to cope with pencils and books; their lives were more attuned to the rake, the plow, and working the stubborn earth. Their teacher, very aware of both their ambitions and their lack of book training, felt frustrated because he could not transform them overnight into scholars. At the end of each school day when Frederick returned to his room he sought the counsel of his God. He felt there must be a way to help his people.

He taught by day and prayed by night. Eventually his entreaties to the Lord became two-way conversations. The Lord answered Frederick Cullen, but at first he would not listen. Then toward the end of his second year of teaching he began to realize that he could no longer ignore this insistent voice. The Lord wanted him, Frederick, to be His representative.

Now his whole being was washed with a wave of relief. He no longer felt guilty about abandoning his pupils at the end of the school year. He was going to do as God willed. Upon the advice of his minister he went back to Baltimore and enrolled in the theological department of Morgan College.

The students of theology at Morgan were assigned to the surrounding country churches as circuit preachers. The pay for these services was supposed to help with their college expenses. However, Frederick's hundred and twenty dollars a year did little to relieve him of financial the cast-off dresses of his older sisters long after he should have graduated to pants. He started to work at an early age. In those days before the turn of the century, a son of former slaves usually had to settle for household work, and so did Fred. There was an advantage to this, however; the nature of his employment enabled him to schedule his work before and after school hours.

The town of Fairmount offered no training for Negro children beyond the elementary school. So when Fred finished the eighth grade he pushed on to Baltimore. There he entered the all-Negro Morgan College. In those days it was customary for such institutions to maintain a high school department for youngsters like Fred who could not get a secondary education in their home towns. Fortunately young Cullen was able to find domestic work in Baltimore, so he stayed at Morgan until he had completed his high school work and enough college courses to qualify him to teach.

During his student days in Baltimore Frederick experienced his religious conversion at a revival meeting. His exhausting tussle at the altar created a noticeable change in his behavior. After that he didn't want to talk about worldly things. He found great comfort in singing the familiar revival hymns as he worked.

His lady employer asked him why he was talking so little and singing so much these days. He replied mysteriously, "There is something within me I cannot explain, something within me that holdeth the reins, something within me, O praise his name, something, something, something, and that something is the Holy Spirit."

5

were warmed by the evidence of her customary good housekeeping. The old-fashioned living room looked comfortable and inviting, and from the kitchen downstairs came the scent of freshly baked bread.

Countee carried his luggage to his study on the third floor. Everything was just as he had left it. The hundreds of books on the shelves seemed to welcome him back, and the sight of his desk made him want to sit down and write a poem. Instead he went over to the window and looked out on Seventh Avenue. Although the grassy strip that divided the broad thoroughfare was still green, there was a hint of fall in the air. Most of the pedestrians had abandoned their leisurely summer pace and were moving along as if they meant business. As he watched them, Countee pushed the memories of Europe out of his mind and began to think of how he could combine his writing with a job.

Downstairs Frederick Asbury Cullen moved about trying to find places for his newly acquired treasures as he described to Carolyn some of the highlights of his trip. He suddenly became keenly aware of the contrast between this comfortable home and the dreary rooms he had occupied during his first year in New York.

Dr. Cullen had come here from his native Maryland in 1902, young, enthusiastic, and almost penniless. His life had been difficult since the day of his birth in the country town of Fairmount. His father had died when Fred, the youngest of eleven children, was only two months old. As a result the boy was often hungry, although his mother did her best to provide for the family. Fred had to wear

4

ize how much he had missed the old familiar surroundings. He was eager to compare notes with his friends who were in the thick of the Negro Renaissance. The vogue for the Negro arts was at its height, and Harlem was the center of the activity. Dr. Alain Locke, Negro author and educator, had just published his book, *The New Negro.* This volume, a compilation of essays, poetry, and stories by and about Negro writers, painters, musicians, sculptors, and teachers, focused attention on the changing pattern of the Negro's contribution to American culture. Of the men and women represented in Dr. Locke's book a majority either lived in Harlem or had regular contacts with this Negro metropolis.

Countee Cullen knew many of these people: Langston Hughes, writer of verse in a rhythmic "blues" style, currently studying at Lincoln University in Pennsylvania, but visiting Harlem at every opportunity; James Weldon Johnson, whose poem, "The Creation: A Negro Sermon," gave promise of becoming a classic; Eric Walrond, writer of colorful realistic fiction; and Alain Locke, himself. Like Countee, some of them would just now be returning to New York from other places.

The Cullens were glad to be back. They lived in the parsonage adjoining Salem Methodist Episcopal Church. The home that the congregation provided for its pastor and his family was a four-storied brownstone house with fourteen rooms. Countee and his father climbed the stone steps and entered the house through the heavy wooden door. Carolyn Belle Cullen, Frederick's wife, was there to greet them. As they followed her through the house they

3

serious-faced officer had to smile when the minister un-stopped one of the bottles and poured out a few drops of the water to prove his innocence. Dr. Cullen also planned to enliven his sermons with firsthand descriptions of the holy places he had seen.

Countee, on the other hand, had lasting impressions of the memorials to Keats and Shelley in Rome, the Wailing Wall in Jerusalem, and the Poets' Corner in Westminster Abbey. He could use these ideas in his writing. At the age of twenty-three he had already published his first book.

When the ship had docked and the Cullens, after some delay, had claimed their baggage and found a taxi, they settled back for the long ride to Harlem. They would have been glad to sit in silence and think about their many experiences, but the cab driver was in a talkative mood. He wanted to know what his passengers thought about Rudolph Valentino, whose death had been front-page news for several days. The cabbie reported that he had run afoul of a crowd of hysterical young women fighting to get into the funeral parlor where the body of the hand-some movie idol lay in state. Excitement had mounted when a rumor arose that the young film star might have been poisoned.

August, 1926, was also the month when New Yorkers had thronged to welcome Gertrude Ederle, the nineteen-year-old swimmer who was the first woman to conquer the English Channel. The cab driver had opinions about this feat, too, but his conversation was cut short by the arrival of his fares at their destination, 2190 Seventh Avenue.

The ride through lower Harlem had made Countee real-

CHAPTER

I

At the end of summer in 1926, Countee Cullen stood on the deck of the *Ile de France* with his adopted father, the Reverend Frederick Asbury Cullen, pastor of the Salem Methodist Church in Harlem. As the liner approached the New York harbor, returning tourists buzzed with talk of the purchases they had to declare to the customs officers. Countee's head was filled with loftier thoughts. He and his father were returning from a tour of Europe and the Holy Land. The trip had been a gift from Salem's members in appreciation of Dr. Cullen's twenty-five years of service to the church.

Both men were bringing back more than just the usual tourist's souvenirs. The preacher had jugs of water from the Jordan River that he intended to mix with the communion wine as a means of sharing his experience with his parishioners. He and his son had been amused at the look on the customs officer's face as he questioned them about the contents of the earthenware vessels. Even the

Illustrations

ACKNOWLEDGMENTS

Harold Jackman
Charles S. Johnson
Percy L. Julian
Charles W. Kirnon
Allen Klots, Jr.
Robert McCullough
Augusta E. Meriwether
Archie Palmer
William Poole
Lula B. Roache
Schomburg Collection
Carl Van Vechten
Yale University Library
Maurice Zolotow

Acknowledgments

For permission to quote passages from Countee Cullen's poems acknowledgment is made to Harper and Row.

Dodd, Mead and Company granted permission to quote from Paul Laurence Dunbar.

For helpful interviews, letters, suggestions, and familial patience, thanks are due to

> Lucille Armistead
> Atlanta University Library
> Arna Bontemps
> Mrs. Countee Cullen
> Countee Cullen Library
> DeWitt Clinton High School
> Jacque J. Ferguson
> James W. Gowins
> Roberta Bosley Hubert
> Langston Hughes
> Indiana University Writers' Conference
> Indianapolis Public Schools

To the memory of my sister, Augusta

Library of Congress Catalog Card Number: 66-24265
Printed in the United States of America
by The Cornwall Press, Inc., Cornwall, N. Y.

Countee Cullen

AND THE

Negro Renaissance

By BLANCHE E. FERGUSON

ILLUSTRATED

Dodd, Mead & Company

NEW YORK

him that a respectable young lady could not keep company with a gentleman until her parents consented. Since she was only visiting Atlantic City, Frederick would have to wait until she returned to her home in Baltimore.

After corresponding for several months with Carolyn Belle, Frederick was invited by her parents to visit them in Baltimore. In her own home Carolyn seemed even more inviting than Frederick had dreamed. The delicious family meal was prepared by her own hands. After dinner she sang informally, accompanying herself on the piano. No setting could have been more suitable for his proposal. He returned to New York an engaged man.

They were married in his New York church by a minister friend before the year ended. Frederick Cullen now began to realize how truly the Lord had blessed him, for he had found the ideal minister's wife.

The parsonage where they set up housekeeping was modest in comparison with the fourteen-room house Salem was able to provide in its later, more affluent years. But the newlyweds were happy to have it. Number 234 West 131st Street was a brown frame building of two stories and English basement, rather less imposing than its brownstone neighbors with their high stoops. It was easily distinguished from them not only by its height but also by a small plot of land in front. In this four-foot square there was room for a small ailanthus tree and a few hardy plants. Inside, the high-ceilinged rooms were comfortable and neat in a prim Victorian way. The dining room was the center of family activity. Here on a dark wood table lay the family Bible, a fourteen-inch-long Morocco-bound book showing signs of constant use. From its well-marked pages Frederick selected passages to introduce the family devotions before each meal.

Salem's membership grew steadily. Soon Frederick Cullen was preaching to a packed auditorium each Sunday in the church that had been made from two adjoining houses on 133rd Street.

One day as Dr. Cullen was on his way to the church to inspect certain facilities, he noticed a man who seemed to be waiting for him. On coming closer he recognized that it was his friend James Gowins, an officer of the church. Gowins obviously had something on his mind, but he did not come out with it right away. They talked about the church finances and the services. Then Gowins complimented the minister on last Sunday's sermon. Finally in a casual tone he asked if Dr. Cullen had ever noticed in the Sunday School a bright-eyed eleven-year-old boy with the odd name of Countee Porter. Frederick Cullen thought a moment and then replied that he did indeed remember the lad.

James Gowins described his first encounter with the child. Countee and another neighbor boy, Lorenzo Albright, had come to the house to play with Gowin's little half-sister, Margaret. Maggie said that Countee was new to the neighborhood and very smart in school. Soon the three children became fast friends and were attending Sunday School together at Salem. Then they began to take part in the Sunday evening programs of the Epworth League (a nationwide young people's society of the Methodist Episcopal Church).

10

One day Gowins went to Harlem Hospital to visit a sick relative. There he saw the little Porter boy. Countee's mother (or the woman Gowins thought was his mother) was seriously ill, and Countee, small as he was, went regularly to the hospital to do what he could to make her comfortable. Gowins was deeply affected by this unusual display of tenderness.

Recently Maggie and Lorenzo had reported that Countee's mother had died and that the boy was staying temporarily with friends. As far as the neighbors knew, he had no close relatives, only some distant kin in Kentucky. Gowins was willing to take the youngster into his own home. But he believed this bright little fellow ought to have a chance at a college education. Gowins could not afford this, so he wondered if Dr. Cullen would consider taking the boy. Gowins was sure the church would help finance Countee's education if he proved worthy.

Frederick Cullen sent for Countee and they had a long talk. He and his wife were impressed with the child's good manners and with the intelligent way he took part in the conversation. Since they had no children of their own, this personable youngster seemed like a gift from God. So they sent him to get his belongings and prepare to live with them. A family friend who was a social worker made the necessary arrangements. They boy even made a trip to Kentucky. But in due time Countee Porter became a Cullen.

Soon after this Dr. Cullen was able to report to James Gowins that his "son" was adjusting beautifully and was already calling Mrs. Cullen "Ma."

CHAPTER

II

Countee Cullen, eleven years old, began a new life in the Salem parsonage. Its religious atmosphere affected him even as a child. At an age when he could hardly have been expected to understand grownups' books he spent many hours poring over the volumes in his father's theological library. By the time he was thirteen he had read practically all of them.

Only a few blocks away was the Harlem branch of the public library, located at 135th Street and Lenox Avenue. This was a busy corner. At regular intervals a dozen or more people emerged from the subway. Often this group included several bewildered Negroes, fresh from the South, who had come to New York to seek a better life. They were readily identified by their cardboard suitcases and other assorted bundles, and by their reluctance to move away from this spot in the center of Harlem.

At some time during the day the pushcart stove of the sweet potato man would appear at this corner with steam rising from a narrow vent, and a glowing bed of coals cooking delicious-smelling yams. The one person who resented the potato man's presence was "Pig Foot Mary." She felt that she had priority on this corner because she did not move her stand from block to block. This was the permanent location where she cooked and sold pigsfeet and boiled corn on the cob. The neighborhood customers, however, impartially patronized both vendors.

Countee knew this corner well because he was a frequent visitor to the library. As he approached the building he often found a group of screaming stickball players partially blocking the entrance. He carefully stacked his books in a corner of the library steps and enviously watched the older boys as they played. Occasionally he had to dodge the sharply flying ball, but sometimes he was able to retrieve it for one of the players.

In contrast to the street outside, the library was cool in summer, warm in winter, and always quiet. The reading room had shiny wooden tables and thousands of books. Presiding over all this was Miss Ernestine Rose. She sat on her throne behind the circulation desk, a queen from the crown of her dark hair coiled in a smooth bun to the soles of her sensible shoes. As Countee approached the desk on one of his regular visits, their eyes would meet in recognition. Then they discussed the books he was returning. Sometimes she agreed with his opinion, but sometimes she did not. He was always free to browse as long as he cared to, for Miss Rose knew that he would never have to be reminded of the rules. When he was leaving, the librarian usually suggested to him a book he might not yet have

13

discovered. He accepted her recommendations with shy politeness and a warm feeling for this kindly woman. She was his friend.

Books were his friends, too. Although he was only eleven years old, he realized this on a particularly important day when he was invited to have his picture made. A photographer friend of the family had asked him to pose. The occasion called for careful preparation. Countee hurried upstairs, skillfully avoiding the tail of the sleepy old family cat who blocked the pathway to his room.

In the bedroom Countee hastened to make ready. Of course, he must wash up thoroughly. What should he wear? He thought of the pictures he had seen in books and the portraits in the museum. Yes, he would have to look dignified. When he heard Ma coming down the hall, he feared that she would not let him wear his "Sunday best." However, to his relief, she did not interfere with his choice. Soon they were calling to him to hurry, for the photographer wanted to use the natural daylight.

It was a simple matter to slip into the clothes that Ma always kept fresh and ready for Sundays. Quickly he leaped over the dozing cat and dashed through the door that banged sharply behind him. He took a deep breath and stood erect before the entrance of his home. He was wearing a hat, a white shirt, and a tie. In his hands he held an open storybook.

Although the Cullens were inclined to overindulge their only child, they did not deny him the companionship of other children, especially that of his cousins, the Bosley girls. These guests may well have been attracted to their young host mainly by the bountiful good food Mrs. Cullen spread before them. The girls enjoyed Countee, of course, but they also stood somewhat in awe of him because he always carried a pad and pencil and made such high marks in school.

His girl cousins sometimes found him over fastidious, and he liked to tease them, too. For example, there is the incident of the pickles. One day the Bosley children took a walk with Countee that led them by a neighborhood delicatessen. Now of all the delicacies displayed in such a store—the pungent sausages, the corned beef, the mysterious salads, the big fat bread rolls, the cheese cakes, the charlotte russe—nothing was more enticing to New York youngsters than the wet, smelly pickle barrel. After taking stock of their finances, the girls saw that they could buy a pickle apiece. They emerged from the store munching contentedly while vinegar oozed slowly down their wrists. Their companion had disappeared! For a moment both girls had the same dreadful thought: they faced scoldings, or worse, from two sets of parents who had repeatedly admonished them to stay together whenever they went adventuring. Now they had lost Countee. But when they finally looked across the street, they saw their cousin in the distance. Breathlessly they ran to catch up, but Countee pretended not to know them. When they reached the house he solemnly informed them that he couldn't bring himself to associate with girls eating pickles in the street. But there was a twinkle in his eye as he spoke.

In summer the Cullens liked to get away from the heat of the city. They had a summer home, first in Maryland,

and later in Pleasantville, New Jersey. In the country Countee liked to write down thoughts that occurred to him and to record observations of things and places he saw. The stay-at-homes among his friends received from him, instead of postcards, long yellow scrolls covered with verses describing the sights and sounds of the country, his visits to the shore, and the progress of the daily croquet games.

In September, activity in the Cullens' parsonage and church was stepped up. During Countee's boyhood, Salem Methodist Episcopal Church stood at the corner of Lenox Avenue and 133rd Street, having been remodeled from two private houses. But its congregation was outgrowing these quarters as fast as it had outgrown the status of a mission and become a church. One of the reasons for this growth was the popularity of the children's recreational program designed to help reduce undesirable Harlem gang activity. But the youngsters also had their place in the regular religious program. Countee was particularly attracted by the Epworth League. There the children had their own choir, conducted devotions, and presented programs. Countee starred as an elocutionist. His specialty was Walt Whitman's "O Captain, My Captain," and as he concluded his number with the noble hero "fallen cold and dead," the audience wept.

September always brought another joy to Countee Cullen—the opening of school. There was the pleasant scramble to get to the classroom on time. It was fun to tumble into the cloakroom with its friendly smell of boys mingled with the varied aromas of newspaper-wrapped lunches

16

and the familiar odor of oilcloth covering their books. Countee loved the march into the assembly room. There under the watchful eye of a stern-faced teacher a boy could suppress a self-conscious giggle and then straighten up manfully for the salute to the flag: "I pledge allegiance to my flag and to the Republic for which it stands." My flag! (The words had not yet been changed to the more impersonal "flag of the United States of America.")

Countee liked school. He took pride in his work, in the neatness of his notebooks. One day he came home proudly carrying his writing certificate. It read: "This certificate for excellence in the Palmer Method of Business Writing is issued to Countee Porter Cullen, May 15, 1915." He was nearing his twelfth birthday now.

School was the jumping-off place for exciting excursions —visits to the great museums, visits to the zoos. A trip to the zoo in Central Park was a real adventure. A sensitive boy felt a kinship with the creatures he saw there: the swinging monkeys, the lordly lions, the varicolored birds, and even the lowly immobile snakes. Reading the labels on the cages he could, in his mind's eye, travel to West Africa, the home of the green monkey; or he could place the blue and yellow macaw in a tree in its native South America. On a warm day he envied Happy, the sea lion, swimming friskily in a wide circle, sloshing water on the pigeons who perched unimpressed on the edge of his pool. Countee watched with interest and began to harbor a feeling of sympathy for these imprisoned beasts.

Other city influences affected him too. Today as we read his cultured, orderly lines, we can look back into

17

Cullen's youth and view him against a slowly moving kaleidoscope. It embraces the stately spires of St. Patrick's Cathedral, the stone façade of the public library with its dignified lions on guard, the unbelievably green grass of Central Park, the twinkling marquees of Broadway theaters, the transplanted sections of other lands, the ghettos, the tenements, the worshippers entering Harlem churches.

Harlem, as Countee knew it, extended from 110th Street north to 155th Street. It was bounded on the east by the Harlem and East rivers and on the west by Amsterdam Avenue. In 1902, when the Reverend Mr. Cullen first arrived in New York, the influx of Negroes to this area had barely begun. They were concentrated in a few streets that had been hastily emptied whenever one house on a block had "gone colored." Before long, however, Harlem ceased to resemble in any way the settlement of peaceful farms established by the Dutch.

Seventh and Lenox avenues became the main thoroughfares of Harlem. They were broad streets on which residents and visitors liked to stroll. On Sundays you could run into anyone you wanted to see if you waited long enough on Seventh Avenue. And as Countee walked along that thoroughfare, he watched the churchgoers leaving the temples of the long-winded preachers, lingering on the steps and sidewalks reluctant to break up their weekly talkfests. The noisiest of them, however, came from the store-front churches. The din they created seemed a compensation for their lack of material possessions. The larger churches released the more affluent and style-conscious.

Countee and his comrades were easily lost in a crowd made up of faces of every hue—pink and white, creamy yellow, brick-tan, chocolate, café au lait, orange, ebony, Strolling past the large apartment houses Countee could see open windows with men and women resting their elbows on pillows and watching the passing parade. Many leaned over the window sills to get a better look and occasionally called out to friends strolling by. At the Lafayette Theater, Countee paused at the entrance to stare at the large glossy photographs of the Lafayette Players. These serious Negro students of acting presented both popular plays of the day and dramas with racial themes. The pictures of stars Rose McClendon, Abbie Mitchell, and Richard "De Lawd" Harrison were familiar to most Harlemites.

The end of the Sunday morning church services was a signal to the cabaret owners that they might open their doors. The music from Baron Wilkins' Club or from Small's Paradise floated out to the strollers on the avenue. Countee knew that "Pa," as he called his father, was violently opposed to these establishments and had, in fact, waged a private war against the owners. Nevertheless he himself was fascinated by the music. He could not understand how a song as moving and rhythmical as the "St. Louis Blues" could be sinful. And he could see nothing wrong in deriving happiness from dancing to the lively tunes composed and played by "Fats" Waller.

Harlem during the first World War had its undertones of unrest. Tales of violence were creeping up from the

19

South, especially from Waco, Texas, from Memphis, Tennessee, and from East St. Louis, Illinois. Some of these stories were apocryphal, but many were not. The Cullen household was now filled with excited talk. Pa and his associates mournfully discussed the latest atrocities. A Negro had been burned to death by an angry mob because it was rumored he had killed a white man. Someone told of having met a group of wide-eyed white children returning from a lynching. Their parents had taken them there as a form of entertainment. When Countee heard some of these stories, he became physically sick.

Reverend Frederick Cullen's indignation reached a climax when he learned about the great disturbance in Houston, Texas. Some Negro soldiers stationed there had been accused of shooting up the town, and several of them had been arrested and hanged. (Countee could visualize a row of khaki-clad bodies hanging from ropes, their ebony faces frozen in grimaces of pain.) Dr. Cullen went into action at once. His committee decided to send a delegation to call on President Wilson in behalf of American Negroes in general, and specifically the imprisoned soldiers in Texas. Frederick Cullen was chosen as one of these ambassadors; their spokesman, however, was to be James Weldon Johnson.

The Cullen parsonage stirred with preparations for Frederick's departure on this important mission. To Countee the activity was a relief from the nightmare of atrocities against colored men.

In Washington the committee spent a half hour with the President. Wilson listened politely to Mr. Johnson's eloquent plea. Presenting a petition with twelve thousand

20

signatures, the spokesman asked executive clemency for the Negro soldiers of the Twenty-fourth Infantry who had been sentenced to death. He said that thirteen men had already been hanged without a chance to appeal to their Commander-in-Chief. He spoke of the unquestioned loyalty of his people and of their deep sorrow over the repeated instances of brutality and unfairness. Then he rested his case.

There followed for the committee tormented days of wondering. Had they said too much? Too little? Would opposing pressures and influences be greater than theirs? Eventually word came that the soldiers had been freed by Executive Order.

It is not surprising that Frederick Cullen was later elected president of the Harlem Branch of the National Association for the Advancement of Colored People. Under his leadership the branch sent a Negro to Geneva, Switzerland, to represent the colored people of America at the League of Nations. The churches of Harlem and a few prosperous individuals helped finance the trip. Everybody agreed that the most brilliant Negro in New York should make the journey. They chose William Edward Burghardt DuBois, Ph.D. He was then editor of *The Crisis*, official magazine of the NAACP. Already he had studied at Fisk, Harvard, and Berlin universities and was the author of several books. He had also taught economics at Atlanta University, a Negro college in Georgia.

While the leaders of Harlem were grappling with their perennial problems, young Countee was involved in a less controversial undertaking, the pursuit of an education.

On February 4, 1918, he enrolled in De Witt Clinton High School, one of New York's secondary schools for boys who wanted a general education that would also prepare them for college entrance. There were other schools for students primarily interested in commercial work or the various trades. And boys and girls did not customarily attend high school in the same building.

To reach De Witt Clinton, Countee had to board the Sixth Avenue elevated train each morning at 130th Street and ride downtown to 59th Street. Then he walked west.

At the corner of Tenth Avenue and 59th Street a building of gray stone and red brick loomed up before him. Its cornerstone read: "De Witt Clinton High School, 1903." After the fashion of the time the building was elaborate. It extended a full city block and housed 2500 boys. Above the arched main entrance perched an American eagle carved in stone. Along the façade at regular intervals were stone carvings of owls and stone figures in cap and gown. The basement and first floor windows were guarded with iron grilles, and the entire structure was surrounded by an iron spiked fence. Going around to the side entrance Countee could look west two blocks to the Hudson River where ferryboats moved toward the Jersey shore. And across the street he could see the ancient red brick buildings of Roosevelt Hospital.

Back at the main entrance Countee joined the crowd of boys climbing the ten stone steps leading to the front door. Overhead they could see the series of turrets that crowned the building and made it look like a medieval castle.

CHAPTER

III

At one o'clock in the afternoon on Thursday, November 7, 1918, classroom work at De Witt Clinton High School came to an abrupt end. Someone had brought in an "extra" purchased from an excited newspaper vendor. The bold headlines proclaimed that the armistice ending the first World War had been signed. Hurriedly the students were assembled to receive the announcement. Their shouts and cheers were quieted long enough for them to sing the "Star Spangled Banner" and the "Marseillaise." Then they were dismissed.

The momentum of a mass of jubilant boys carried Countee through the doors and onto the sidewalk outside the school. Already people were gathering in the streets. Some were shouting; others were quietly pressing their way toward their homes or other destinations. An elderly lady just stood still and murmured, "Peace, peace," as the tears streamed down her cheeks. Sirens screamed and bells sounded. Strangers began to embrace each other.

Storekeepers locked their doors and joined in the celebration. None of these people knew that their rejoicing was premature, that they were the victims of a false report, and that the real armistice would not be signed until the following Monday. Hours later one drunken man, when informed by a police officer that the war was not over yet, replied that he expected it would end sometime. He intended to keep celebrating until the great day arrived.

Countee and his friend Bob made their way toward Harlem. They would not go to the library today. Ordinarily the Harlem branch library was the after-school gathering place of those nonathletes who loved to read. It was almost like a club. Today Countee bypassed not only the library but also the YMCA where Bob made his home. He directed his steps toward the parsonage.

His parents welcomed him in a state of gratitude. It was almost as if he were a returning warrior. Ma was happy for the mothers who no longer needed to fear for the safety of their soldier sons. Pa was grateful that the sacrifices of the Negro heroes of this "war to end all wars" had not been in vain. There were embraces and prayers and rejoicing. Countee began to wonder what it would mean for the world to be at peace again. Already a poem was forming in his mind.

This poem came to fruition as a two-part composition called "Christmas—1917 and 1919." It had grown within him for a year, and on completion it was published in the Christmas issue of *The Magpie*, Clinton's literary magazine. It was one of the many contributions that Countee made to his high school's publications.

During his first year at De Witt Clinton High School, Countee Cullen wrote little poetry because he was trying for high marks in his classwork. But on a day in May, 1918, when he was not yet fifteen years old, he sat reading an educational magazine, *The Modern School*. His brown eyes were glued to the page. Suddenly over his sensitive, slender face there came a smile of satisfaction, but as he looked away for a moment, his eyes were filled with wonder. Could it be possible that he was reading his own poem, "To the Swimmer?" He turned back to the page and read again the closing lines:

> My heart goes out to you of dauntless courage
>   and spirit indomitable,
> And though my lips would speak, my spirit
>   forbids me to ask,
> "Is your heart as true as your arm?"

He had written this poem more than a year ago as an assignment in Mr. Cronyn's class at Townsend Harris High School. Countee had enrolled in the ninth grade there before transferring to Clinton. The actual composition had not been too difficult. Mr. Cronyn believed that a boy could create many things, among them poetry, and Countee Cullen had performed his task and forgotten it.

But George Cronyn had not forgotten. For two years, hampered by some curious and unorthodox beliefs, he had taught in a New York public high school. His notions were considered odd because they included faith in the beauty lying dormant in children. Insisting that the young ones had the ability to create "priceless bits of literature," he encouraged them to write. He prodded their imagination and hoarded their precious compositions.

Then Cronyn happened to read a pamphlet written by a college professor. The author had developed a scale for measuring quality in English compositions. He had selected some samples of writing and arranged them according to his estimation of their literary worth. By using this scale any English teacher could compare his pupils' compositions with the numbered selections and arrive at an evaluation.

"Stuff and nonsense," said George Cronyn to himself angrily. Who was to say that the professor's samples were superior to the gems composed by his own ninth-grade boys?

Cronyn sat down and wrote an article of his own. It was published in *The Modern School,* a monthly magazine "devoted to libertarian ideas in education." In it he blasted the professor's theory. He told how he tried to develop children's attitudes instead of teaching form and content. He offered to pit the efforts of his boys against the most highly rated sample on the professor's scale. Triumphantly he presented two poems composed by high school freshmen as classroom exercises. One of these poems was "To the Swimmer."

As the teen-aged Countee Cullen read his first published poem, he discovered that he could write, and he resolved to do so. The story of his life is a record of the fulfillment of that resolution. It is a record of the joyful adventure he found in lyrical expression. It is also a record of the sorrows and disappointments that such an adventure is bound to bring.

At De Witt Clinton High School, Countee found his race no handicap even though the student body was predominantly white. There were seldom more than two or three colored boys in his classes, and sometimes he was the only Negro. But he enjoyed learning and was an excellent student. He stood well in his class all through high school and was graduated with a 92 percent average, among the top 25 in a class of 600 students.

Latin was one of his favorite subjects. The declensions and conjugations appealed to his orderly mind, and he found the classical myths and adventure stories highly exciting. At first his classmates were awed by his competence. Then one by one they discovered that good old Cullen was willing to share his knowledge. He had an uncanny way of anticipating just what the teacher wanted, and he could show you how to put your translation together so that it really made sense. Soon, however, his kindness and ability began to create a problem for him. He did not like to disappoint his classmates; yet how was he to spare the time to help them?

His Latin teacher found a solution. He guided the generous Countee into a program where his talents could be used with the greatest efficiency. At Clinton a group of Help Classes had been organized to assist backward and deficient students. They were tutored by their more competent classmates, and all the officers were students. Countee, happy for the after-school association with his fellow pupils, was appointed assistant chairman for Latin. Later he became assistant superintendent of the entire Help Classes Organization.

A more surprising aspect of his leadership came in the area of discipline. One of the Clinton teachers decided that a group of carefully chosen students could keep order in the halls of Clinton. The teacher established and gave his name to the Dotey Squad, which became the chief disciplinary organization of the school. Only the brightest pupils were chosen for this force organized along military lines. Dotey boys spent their nonclass periods stationed in strategic positions in the halls, library, and lunch room. The quiet, mild-mannered Cullen, wearing the badge of a Dotey lieutenant, was respected and obeyed.

Countee had been reluctant to accept a place on the squad because he wanted the friendship of his schoolmates. So he was pleasantly surprised to find that they did not resent his position. Soon he found himself being invited to join the debating society and other school clubs. Here again he was usually the only Negro. And a few of his white classmates even invited him to their homes.

Soon after the publication of "To the Swimmer," Countee became acquainted with the school literary magazine, *The Magpie*. He and the staff of this publication developed a close and lasting relationship. His first contribution was an ambitious piece called "Song of the Poets." Occupying a full page it was a series of verses in which Countee gave his impression of certain English and American poets. He had read works of the writers usually studied in school and had described each one in a pungent phrase. He called Lord Byron "the passion poet," Tennyson "chronicler of gallant deeds," Whittier "the Quaker poet," Longfellow "the children's poet," and Poe "the atheist."

There was another American, however, whose verses Countee read with personal pride. He was Paul Laurence Dunbar, a Negro poet of the late nineteenth century. At this stage in his schooling Countee had not heard of any established colored poets. Now he was glad to discover that there was a Negro whose poetic ability had been recognized as worthy of a place in some anthologies of American verse.

Like Cullen, Dunbar had begun his writing career as a student in high school. At his home in Dayton, Ohio, he edited his high school newspaper. After his graduation he went on to produce several volumes of verse, some short stories, essays, and novels. Although he wrote many poems in legitimate English, people seemed to associate him mainly with his verse written in dialect.

Negro elocutionists popular during Countee's childhood usually included Dunbar's "In the Morning" in their repertories. This humorous poem depicts a mother's efforts to get her lazy son, Lias, out of bed in the morning. In many Negro homes mothers began to use the opening lines of this poem as a reveille for their sleepy children. "Lias, Lias, bless de Lawd/Don't you know de day's abroad?" a frustrated mother would chant. And the children would giggle and repeat the lines gleefully.

Countee had difficulty in reading those poems that

Dunbar had written in dialect. But the poet's other lyrical verses in pure English reached the boy's heart. How true for a shy, sensitive person were these lines:

> Why should the world be over-wise,
> In counting all our tears and sighs?
> Nay, let them only see us, while
> We wear the mask.

Then there was Dunbar's expression of sympathy for an imprisoned bird:

> It is not a carol of joy or glee,
> But a prayer that he sends from his heart's
> deep core,
> But a plea, that upward to Heaven he flings—
> I know why the caged bird sings!

As Countee read Dunbar a warm feeling of kinship flowed over him. So in his "Song of the Poets" he saluted Paul Laurence Dunbar as "heart's brother and blood brother."

Cullen's early contributions to *The Magpie* earned him the position of associate editor. His two dozen poems covered a wide variety of subjects and moods. Indeed, whenever a poem was needed, the *Magpie* staff knew that "Tay" could be counted on to come up with one. The nickname was derived from the second syllable of Countee's name. It had been pinned on him by his teasing staff-mates because he insisted on correcting them when they pronounced it "tee."

In January, 1921, a very special poem appeared in *The Magpie*. It was "I Have a Rendezvous with Life" by

Countee Cullen. The story behind this poem is interesting. The setting is World War I. In 1914, three years before the United States entered the war, a young American named Alan Seeger, who had been living and writing in France for a couple of years, decided to join the French Foreign Legion. While he was at the front, he composed a poem, "I Have a Rendezvous with Death." It proved to be tragically prophetic, for Seeger was killed in battle in 1916. The popularity of this poem was overwhelming. Among the many who were touched by it was an English teacher at De Witt Clinton High School.

Countee sat on the edge of his seat and listened as his teacher read the beautiful words of doom. He knew, however, that these words were not really for him. He himself wanted to be involved in the adventures of living, both sweet and bitter. So he knew he had to write an answer. That answer was "I Have a Rendezvous with Life (with apologies to Alan Seeger)." Although his poem did not match Alan Seeger's in popularity, it did remarkably well for the work of a boy in his teens.

Countee himself was astounded at the reception of his poem. True, he had entered it in a competition for high school writers sponsored by a women's organization; but no one was more surprised than he when he won first prize. Then things really began to happen. The poem was printed, of course, in the daily papers. People began quoting it. Teachers read it to their classes. Ministers read it to their congregations. Everybody appeared fascinated by this message from a fifteen-year-old boy who believed that living a life was more important than waiting for death.

The Cullens returned from their annual Maryland vacation just after Labor Day in 1921. Countee noticed that Harlem seemed even more colorful than usual. Rain-streaked black, red, and green bunting decorated a number of stores and houses in the vicinity of 135th Street and Lenox Avenue. Groups of two or three men in dark uniforms stood on corners or joined the strollers on the avenue. Some of them wore green and red plumes on their black military hats. Occasionally he saw women dressed as nurses with black crosses on their caps and sleeves. And here and there a bandsman carried his shiny brass instrument.

Countee soon realized that he was looking at the stragling remains of the convention that had been held during the month of August by the Universal Negro Improvement Association. This organization had been founded by Marcus Garvey, a native of the British West Indies. He had come to New York to start a movement of protest against the way black people were being treated all over the world. In Liberty Hall, a low barn-like building in Harlem, thousands of Negroes had answered his call to an international convention. Visitors came from the West Indies, Africa, Europe, Central America, and Canada. New Yorkers attended the meetings in droves. Many of them agreed wholeheartedly with Garvey's preachments. Others came out of curiosity. And some came merely to scoff or to be entertained.

There was no doubt that Garvey was an accomplished showman. He was a short, plump man with a belligerent, round, black face. But he was resplendent in his gold-braided uniform and large plumed hat. And he was a passionate orator, inspiring his listeners with the belief that a united black front could be a powerful influence in the world. To supplement his vocal appeal he provided the ritual and regalia that his less educated followers liked so well.

Garvey felt that the Negro peoples of the world could establish a great nation on the African continent. His "Back to Africa" slogan provided colored New Yorkers with a host of jokes. Many of Countee's young friends enjoyed making pleasantries about Garveyism. They kidded each other about booking passage on the Back Star Line. They spoke of swinging with the monkeys and running from the lions in Africa. But Pa looked with disfavor on this form of ridicule. He believed Garvey was sincere and courageous, and while he himself did not choose to join the movement, he insisted that Marcus Garvey deserved respect.

Dr. Cullen was not alone in his appraisal. A few months after the UNIA convention, *The Nation* carried an article on the Garvey Movement. It was written by William Pickens, a Phi Beta Kappa Yale graduate, former dean of Morgan College, and Field Secretary for the NAACP. In his essay Pickens said that Garveyism was no laughing matter and that Americans would do well to study the movement and its implications.

* * *

September, 1921, marked the beginning of Countee's last semester at Clinton. By now he had become one of the school's outstanding students. Frederick and Carolyn Cullen were among their son's most enthusiastic devotees. Their pride in his progress in school had been growing with every report card. The publicity he received in connection with "Rendezvous" had strengthened their belief that he might be talented. Of course, there had been earlier signs of his poetic inclination. Even before the publication of "To the Swimmer," Countee had made a game of writing little verses to be sung to popular tunes. Ma with her musical training had been indulgent of these efforts, but now she began to feel that the boy's writing should be taken more seriously.

Countee's parents read each issue of *The Magpie* as soon as he brought the magazine home. By the time young Cullen had reached his senior year in high school they had formed the habit of looking forward to seeing his work in print. His poems often appeared on pages decorated with drawings or designs by Clinton's most talented art students.

Dr. Cullen had more than one reason to be interested in *The Magpie* for January, 1922. First, it contained a poem called "Dad" in which Countee described his adopted father with the keen insight of a teen-ager. It was an apt description of the "circumspect" conservative man whose wise words of advice his son respected. Yet Countee was aware that he himself had to be free to commit the normal follies of youth. He said:

34

And I must follow, follow, follow
The lure of a silver horn,
That echoes out a leafy hollow
Where the dreams of youth are born.

But a gleam in his father's eye assured him that this man had himself once known the sins of boyhood. So the young poet ended with the promise that when his period of discovery had spent itself he would be content to

... turn like dad, and like him win
The peace of a snug arm-chair.

The January *Magpie* also contained tributes to the mid-year graduates. A descriptive line about "Tay" read: "He stuck his finger in every pudding."

As Countee read this tribute to his versatility, he reviewed his years at Clinton with mixed emotions. He felt a modest pride in his accomplishments; yet he regretted leaving this place. Here he had received encouragement in the work he most wanted to do. No one had belittled his attempts to write poetry. He was graduating as class vice-president, an office that customarily went to an outstanding athlete. He had been elected to Arista, the honor society. He was chairman of the Senior Publications Committee, editor-in-chief of the *Cinton News*, associate editor of *The Magpie*, and treasurer of the Inter–High School Poetry Association. He had also won first place in an oratorical contest.

Countee had wanted a successful high school career as much for his parents' sake as for his personal gratification. He was glad, too, that Salem's congregation could be proud of him. The church members felt that in a sense he belonged to them; and true to James Gowins' prediction, they stood ready to give any financial assistance he might need in furthering his education should his father's salary prove insufficient.

As matters stood now, he was all set to enter the college that his teachers at Clinton had recommended—New York University.

CHAPTER

IV

F$_{AR}$ $_{AWAY}$ from De Witt Clinton High School lies University Heights in the Bronx where one of the five campuses of New York University is located. By the time Countee reached his destination each day, the subway train that he rode to his classes had already emerged from its underground tracks and was swaying along on elevated rails. From the platform at University Avenue and 181st Street, Countee could see the spacious grounds surrounding the college of arts and science. This was to be his academic home for three and a half years. Here he immersed himself in literary studies, warming especially to the nineteenth-century English poets, most particularly to Keats. During his undergraduate career he was to add courses in French, Latin, Greek, German, philosophy, and education.

Countee was quick to discover some of the extra benefits of college matriculation. He found that as a student he could buy tickets at reduced rates for the concerts at

Carnegie Hall and the thrilling performances at the Metropolitan Opera House. He enjoyed attending these events with fellow students, and he regaled his parents with vivid accounts of the things he had seen and heard.

Another asset of the university was its well-stocked library. In this cool stone building Countee found, as usual, that he felt at home with the librarians. Every member of the staff recognized the familiar face of Cullen, one of their most regular patrons. At first they knew him only as a stationary figure seated in his accustomed place and absorbed in his books. Then one day Cullen entered the room with a special bounce in his walk and a grin on his face. Standing at the circular desk he reached into his pocket to draw out a newspaper clipping which he handed to the librarian. She read it in silence and then beckoned excitedly to her co-worker. Then and there the three of them held a little celebration. Countee Cullen had just had a poem accepted by *The New York Times*.

As he sat at his favorite study table in the library basking in his good fortune, Countee looked out at a broad green commons. Perhaps this expanse of grass reminded him of the blue grass of Kentucky, a memory that had lain dormant in him since the time when he had visited that state as a young boy. There he had heard a ballad about a brown girl. She was a beautiful creature who vied with a fair London maiden for the love of a handsome lord. The brown girl won him in marriage. In true gory ballad style the triangle ended in death for all three participants. This was poetic justice for the mother of the groom, who had advised her son to marry the brown girl because of her material possessions.

The tale stayed with Countee, but he didn't do anything about it until his sophomore year at New York University. Then he wrote it out as a literary ballad. That year his "Ballad of the Brown Girl" won second prize in the Witter Bynner undergraduate poetry contest sponsored by the Poetry Society of America. His awareness of what was going on around him as a boy had finally paid off, or so it seemed. But after the poem had been published, Countee learned that the brown girl of the original old English ballad was not a colored girl, as he had supposed. The term was merely used to identify her as a peasant.

Despite his misinterpretation the ballad brought him some rewards in addition to the poetry prize. It led to an association with Witter Bynner, himself. It also prompted the writing of one of the most highly prized letters that Countee had ever received. This letter came from the outstanding authority on ballads, Professor Lyman Kittredge of Harvard. Countee found it hard to believe Dr. Kittredge had written that "Ballad of the Brown Girl" was the finest literary ballad he had ever read!

Although Countee was certainly aware of his race, his love of learning and the joy of writing some successful poems probably kept him from being militant about racial injustices. All around him Negro writers were turning out protest articles such as the one written by Eric Walrond in *The New Republic* in November, 1922. Under the title "On Being Black" Walrond gave examples of the kind of discrimination particularly offensive to the Negro intellectual. He spoke of his experience in a store where he wanted to buy a pair of goggles. The clerk insisted on selling him a particular style, and when Walrond hesitated, the seller presented what he considered a sure-fire recommendation. He said he sold these goggles to all the colored chauffeurs. Since he was not a chauffeur, Walrond left indignantly.

Another instance of discrimination occurred when Walrond was seeking a stenographic job. After being first ignored, then given evasive answers, he was finally recommended to a prospective employer on Lenox Avenue. This man turned out to be one of his own former pupils.

Finally the writer told of his attempt to buy passage for his wife on a steamer to Kingston, Jamaica. He had seen an advertisement announcing a special rate. But at the ticket office he was informed that the rate applied only to cabins for three persons. To obtain the bargain tickets, he was told, his wife must find two other colored passengers to share the stateroom.

Countee knew that such experiences were common. But he did not join the active crusade. He stuck to his classes and his poetry.

At NYU Cullen was frankly, though quietly, ambitious. He owed it to his parents to make good grades, but since he liked to study, this was no problem. With his poetry, however, he was aiming for recognition by publication in the literary magazines. His goal would be reached only after hard work—writing, revising, polishing—and the inevitable rejection slips. Many people might have been silenced by discouragement, but Countee had things to say and wanted to say them.

In November of his sophomore year his efforts were rewarded. *The Bookman* accepted and published his poem, "To a Brown Boy." It was a short poem, only three four-line stanzas. But in it he had dared to be sensual. He began:

> That brown girl's swagger gives a twitch
> To beauty like a queen;
> Lad, never dam your body's itch
> When loveliness is seen.

He continued his plea for the unashamed acceptance of one's natural impulses:

> For there is ample room for bliss
> In pride in clean, brown limbs,
> And lips know better how to kiss
> Than how to raise white hymns.
>
> And when your body's death gives birth
> To soil for spring to crown,
> Men will not ask if that rare earth
> Was white flesh once, or brown.

He was now on his way.

In the following year, 1924, it seemed that no literary magazine could bear to go to press without a Countee Cullen poem. But 1923 had a unique importance in Countee's life. It marked the beginning of what might be called the era of Yolande.

While Countee was a student at NYU, Nina Yolande DuBois was attending Fisk University in Nashville, Tennessee. She was following a family tradition since her father, William Edward Burghardt DuBois, had spent his undergraduate days at Fisk. Yolande, a pleasant-faced brown girl, was majoring in art. Although her lively disposition and social sense undoubtedly attracted many friends on the campus, some of her schoolmates were frankly curious to know her simply because of her family background.

She was the only daughter of a man whose intellect and militancy had made him perhaps the best known and most highly respected Negro of his time. He had earned his Ph.D. at Harvard and had studied in Germany. A Negro of mixed blood, he was a scholarly-looking man with chiseled features and a distinguishing Vandyke beard. His career was marked by a consuming interest in Negro affairs. He was intermittently a college professor, a founder of the Pan African Congress, and author of a dozen or more books. When his daughter enrolled at Fisk, he was serving the NAACP as editor of the organization's magazine, *The Crisis.*

The DuBois parents had lost a son in infancy, so they centered their attention on Yolande. The family lived, during Yolande's early childhood, on the campus of Atlanta University where Dr. DuBois was a professor of economics and history. In this closed community the little girl was well pampered by students and adults. Later when the family moved to New York, Yolande was enrolled in the predominantly white Ethical Culture School there. Then her father decided she should go abroad for her high school education. So her mother took her to England where, after two years, the United States' entry into World War I made it necessary for them to come home.

So Yolande completed her secondary education at Girls' High in Brooklyn, and then went on to Fisk.

The Cullens and DuBoises were well known to each other because of the civic activities of the fathers. Countee was one of the young men who were welcomed as friends by Miss DuBois and her parents. On many an evening in their comfortable living room the young poet held the attention of his listeners as he read from his yet unpublished works. His early practice in elocution, the lyrical quality of his poetry, and his natural flair for reading aloud made these occasions memorable.

At Fisk, Yolande remembered those evenings. Her campus friends discussed with her the progress of the up-and-coming young writer. Yolande was likely to be stopped at any time on the steps of the ivied old Jubilee Hall for a conversation about Cullen. And in the dorm the coeds read his poems together and indulged in envious girl talk about Yolande's good fortune in knowing a real live poet. When news reached the campus that Countee's poem, "Ballad of the Brown Girl," had won a prize in the Witter Bynner contest, the excitement grew to a fever. There had been seven hundred competitors from sixty-three colleges!

Yolande's attention in her lecture classes began to waver. She daydreamed of a brown-eyed poet whose lines were addressed exclusively to her. Could it be that she was the brown girl whose eyes were "black as night is black" and whose mouth was "one red cherry clipt in twain"? She could heard his voice "slow-fluting like a reed." (How applicable to his own reading were the words

43

he had used in one of his poems to describe the tones of another!)

For his part, Countee looked forward to the school vacations. He took his chances at getting dates with the popular Yolande. She enjoyed the fact that he was an attentive and knowledgeable escort at dances and parties. Yet some of their most pleasant moments were spent in the country. There were picnics and excursions to Maryland, nearby New Jersey, and the larger parks around New York. Countee had an open eye for a sheltering tree to lie under or a small hill to climb for a pretty view. Nor was he ever at a loss for words—a story to tell or a poem to read with romantic tenderness. In a group he could be bright and merry, joking and teasing and provoking gales of laughter.

Inevitably the short summer came to an end and it was time for them to return to their respective colleges.

Countee Cullen's success now was incredible and enough to make a young man's head swim. A junior in college, he saw within a span of seven months his poetry in print in eight of the country's leading magazines. In May, 1924, *Poetry* published two pages of his poems: "Simon the Cyrenian Speaks," his tribute to the black man who carried the cross for Christ, and three short "Epitaphs" somewhat reminiscent of Edgar Lee Masters. In the same month his prize poem from high school days, "I Have a Rendezvous with Life," showed up in *Current Opinion*. Other poems were accepted by *Century*, *Harper's*, *The Bookman*, *The American Mercury*, and *The Nation*.

44

Encouraged by his good fortune, Countee began to think in earnest about the possibility of publishing a book of verse. He already had a nucleus, and he would continue to write and polish and revise.

While the press of his classes and his growing career as a writer were keeping Countee occupied, his parents were having a busy time, too. In June of 1924, the Reverend Mr. Cullen experienced what any pastor would consider a crowning achievement in his ministry. He was moving his congregation to a larger, more elegant church. To be sure, the building was not new; but it was certainly an improvement over the old remodeled dwellings in which his flock had previously been housed.

The new Salem was located on Seventh Avenue near 129th Street. The gray stone building had been occupied by Calvary Methodist Episcopal Church, a white congregation. For $285,000 Calvary had sold the church to its colored brethren. Unblinkingly Mr. Cullen undertook this tremendous financial burden, confident of the help of his loyal followers in meeting the monthly payments.

Countee was only one of the many parishioners who were impressed by the large auditorium with its circular seating plan, a brass-railed balcony, and three Gothic stained-glass windows. From the choir loft he could hear the plaintive harmonies of the faithful volunteer singers enhancing Carolyn Cullen's warm solo voice. Sitting in a dark mahogany pew Countee listened to the mellow tones of the fine old pipe organ, background for the familiar litanies of the Church. Here he continued to be bathed in the Biblical lore and tradition that crept into his verses.

45

Some of these verses pleased Dr. Cullen very much. His faith in his son's ability was increasing to the extent that he was willing for Countee to consider writing as a vocation if this was what the boy really wanted. Countee appreciated his father's expression of confidence. He knew that many family sacrifices were necessary for the kind of education he was getting. So on his own he decided to spend a part of each summer vacation as a waiter in Atlantic City, only a few minutes ride from the Cullens' summer place in Pleasantville. Thus he was able to help with his college expenses.

Countee was beginning to meet literary people and to be accepted by them as a young poet of promise. Already the distinguished Witter Bynner had become his friend and advisor. About this same time an auspicious event propelled him into other important acquaintanceships.

At the ornate Rockland Palace, Harlem's newest ballroom, the National Association for the Advancement of Colored People held its annual ball. This was a grand occasion for everybody who was anybody, and for those who aspired to be somebody, and for the nobodies who only hoped to spend a few hours in the shadows of greatness. Glittering lights revolved to spotlight the elegant gowns of the women, and the biracial crowd made valiant efforts to talk politely above the music of the jazz orchestras.

Mr. and Mrs. James Weldon Johnson had brought as their guest Carl Van Vechten, the writer. A native of Cedar Rapids, Iowa, he had graduated from the University of Chicago. Then he became a journalist, working for a time as a foreign correspondent. In New York he created a stir with his writing, first as music critic for *The New York Times,* and later as author of forthright (and sometimes unpopular) articles and a controversial book.

Van Vechten had talent, money, influence, an intelligent interest in the arts, and a deep-seated liberalism in racial matters. He once gently rebuked an interviewer for referring to his "interest in the Negro." To him the phrase implied an artificial pose. Relaxing in a colorful Chinese jacket worn with blue slacks that matched his eyes, he told of a childhood in which he early learned to respect all people, regardless of race. He recalled that the Negro servants in his home were known to him only as Mr. _____ and Mrs. _____. He had been amazed to discover that in other homes children addressed such employees by their given names. Van Vechten also reported with pride that his father had donated money and advice for the establishment of the Piney Woods school for Negro students in Mississippi.

James Weldon Johnson was himself a respected writer of great competence. He was held in esteem by members of his race for many reasons, one of them being his co-authorship with his brother, J. Rosamond Johnson, of "Lift Every Voice and Sing," the so-called Negro national anthem. Johnson, too, was interested in aspiring Negro writers; that is why he made it a point to introduce some of them that night to Carl Van Vechten. Two of the fortunate ones singled out were Langston Hughes and Countee Cullen.

Countee's natural modesty and shyness may have given Van Vechten the impression that he was aloof. In any event the Iowan did not immediately warm to him. He had already read some of Cullen's poetry and considered it good in spite of what he called its derivative quality. He frowned on Cullen's affinity with the classics and the English poets. On the other hand, he found Langston Hughes natural and original, deriving from no source except perhaps the blues.

Nevertheless, Mr. Van Vechten offered to help both young men with personal encouragement and assistance in finding publication. Surprisingly enough Countee did not jump at Van Vechten's offer to intercede with his own publisher. Although this show of pride irritated Van Vechten somewhat, he had to admire Countee's spirit of in dependence.

The National Association for the Advancement of Colored People was not alone in its efforts to promote young writers. Headquartered on Twenty-third Street in Manhattan was the Urban League, another organization devoted to the solution of Negro problems. Its objectives might be summed up in its slogan, "Opportunity," which also became the title of its official magazine. The League organized a series of Opportunity Dinners to introduce young writers to established literary figures. These men read manuscripts of the novices and tried to help them. At the dinners there were usually close to a hundred persons of letters. Through this medium Countee met Frederick Lewis Allen, literary scout for the publishing firm of Harper and Brothers. A fortunate meeting it was, for through it he found a publisher on his own merit.

Cullen's senior year at New York University was even more productive than the one that preceded it. He was

48

published in more than a dozen top-flight magazines. His scholastic achievement was crowned in March by election to Phi Beta Kappa. He was one of eleven students to win membership in his college's chapter of this fraternity, the highest academic honor available to an undergraduate. But it seemed a strange commentary on the times that a New York daily newspaper reported this event with headlines and a lead paragraph devoted to Cullen, the only Negro elected. Not until the third paragraph of the story were the names of the other ten students mentioned.

As a dizzying climax to Cullen's last year at the university, Harper and Brothers contracted to publish his first book, *Color*. The seventy-four poems in this little volume were once described by Helen Keller, the celebrated blind and deaf writer, as being "full of the ardent color of youthful emotions." About a third of the verses touched on racial themes—the tragedy and frustrations of the American Negro, and his colorful African heritage. But the majority of the poems dealt with the nonracial emotions the author experienced as a person and with his observations of the human race. The twenty-nine brief epitaphs (most of them only four lines long) were witty comments on human foibles. They involved the cynic, the poet, the virgin, the atheist, the preacher, the skeptic, the fool, the wanton. There were also epitaphs written for specific individuals—John Keats, Paul Laurence Dunbar, and Joseph Conrad. However, the most quoted of these pseudo tombstone inscriptions was the one Countee called "For a Lady I Know."

> She even thinks that up in heaven
> Her class lies late and snores,

While poor black cherubs rise at seven
To do celestial chores.

As might be expected of a young poet, Countee included several poems on the subject of love, both fulfilled and unrequited. And in his verses he also explored the mysteries of death.

Not even his college graduation meant as much to Countee as the publication of *Color*. In his mind he reviewed the preparation that had led to this day. He thought of the little verses he had scribbled as a child. He remembered "To the Swimmer," the only poem he had ever written in free verse. Although this form was becoming increasingly popular, he did not pursue it, for he did not really like it. Once he listed for a reporter some of the free verse poetry that he considered good. The list included "Silences" by Edgar Lee Masters and "Patterns" by Amy Lowell. For himself he preferred conventional form. He often said that poetry came out of him "metered and rhymed." His poems were proof of this, and he was glad. He was proud, too, of the diligence that had forced him to rewrite each line until it was as perfect as he could make it. He remembered the rejection slips and balanced them against the list of acknowledgments in his first book; seventeen major periodicals had accepted poems and then had given him permission to reprint. He thought ruefully of his earlier determination to be a nonracial poet and wondered why his deepest emotions sprang from the fact that he was a Negro. He reflected upon the Cullens, Ma and Pa, and the debt he owed them. Dedicating the book to them was, he felt, meager payment.

Countee's was one of the young voices making themselves heard in what was now being called the Negro Renaissance. A new spirit had begun to permeate the Negro masses, and a new crop of writers emerged as their spokesmen. These young people believed that the day of the Negro stereotype—the grinning, shuffling, indolent clown—was gone. These writers of the 1920's wanted to become a part of the American scene, and they wanted to get there on the artistic merit of their work.

Countee Cullen was an early inspiration to this group because of his youth and because of the prestige that publication in the top magazines had given him. But others were rapidly climbing to the top, also. There was Claude McKay, whose bitter, emphatic verse could not fail to impress the reader. The poetry of Langston Hughes was rich in the folk idiom which he handled with beauty and originality. Arna Bontemps contributed both poetry and prose. In the field of fiction, Jean Toomer's *Cane* set the pace for the Negro novelist, while the stories of Walter White, Rudolph Fisher, and Jessie Redmon Fauset portrayed the Negro with a new realism.

Fortunately for these writers the ground had been broken by a few hardy pioneers such as W. E. B. DuBois, Alain LeRoy Locke, and James Weldon Johnson. These men, all literary figures in their own right, were active in the movement to encourage new writers. They helped by arranging for the young artists to meet each other and to form contacts with white authors, publishers, and potential sponsors. In these meetings and discussions Countee Cullen was an interested participant.

CHAPTER

V

THE SUMMER AIR in 1925 was filled with talk about evolution. New Yorkers who had never heard of Dayton, Tennessee, now focused their attention on this little town where in July the Scopes Trial began. *The New York Times* became, for its readers, a serialized drama. In its pages they followed the trial of the young teacher who had defied Tennesssee law to teach the theory of evolution. But his fate held less dramatic interest than the colorful personalities of the opposing lawyers. Fundamentalists lined up on the side of the balding, taut-lipped William Jennings Bryan in his fight to protect the Bible from the scientists. On the other hand, the fiery "old lion," Clarence Darrow, had his adherents among the evolutionists.

The average citizen believed he now had to choose either a literal acceptance of the Biblical story of creation or admission of his kinship to the apes. But many people were disturbed by an incident connected with John

Scopes' indictment. In the neighboring state of Kentucky, Miss Lela Scopes, a mathematics teacher, had openly expressed her sympathy with the stand taken by her brother. As a result of her attitude she was dismissed from her position by the school authorities. Incensed by this declaration of "guilt by association," the American Federation of Teachers immediately started an investigation. The attendant publicity was effective. Within a week Lela Scopes was offered a teaching position in Tarrytown, New York.

In the midst of this lively period of controversy Countee Cullen prepared to enter Harvard's graduate school. He had strong incentives for his choice. Many famous men had gone there, including United States presidents. But other alumni closer to Countee's own life had inspired him even more. Dr. Alain Locke, one of the men whom Countee admired most, had studied at the famous Ivy League school. Back in 1907, before Countee was old enough to know what a college was, Alain Locke had taken his bachelor's degree at Harvard. Later he had attended Oxford University in England as a Rhodes Scholar from his native Pennsylvania. Then in 1918 he won his Ph.D. from Harvard.

Countee's association with Dr. Locke had begun while young Cullen was at NYU writing verses and having them accepted by literary magazines. He had visited Howard University in Washington, D.C., while Dr. Locke was a professor there. Countee had never met a more scholarly person than this Negro with the high intellectual forehead and the beautiful, flowing language. Alain Locke, in turn, had high regard for Countee as a poet who "blended the simple with the sophisticated so originally as almost to put the vineyards themselves into his crystal goblets." So when Locke was chosen to edit the Harlem number of *Survey Graphic* in March, 1925, he was pleased to include some of the poetry of his young friend.

Countee was also exposed to the influence of another Harvard graduate—Yolande's father, Dr. DuBois, who likewise had earned two degrees at the celebrated university. The latest was his Ph.D. in 1895. DuBois had since written in his distinctive poetical prose several of the books that were still being read with admiration. They included *The Souls of Black Folk*, an eloquent statement of the condition and aspirations of the Negro, and *The Quest of the Silver Fleece*, a novel.

The effect of Countee's personal contact with Harvard alumni was heightened by the general respect of his associates for the oldest American university. Of course, the Cullens knew there was more to a Harvard education than prestige. They wanted the best for Countee because they believed he had the ability to profit from the finest training. Salem was now paying Dr. Cullen a good enough salary to enable him to see his son through a year of graduate study. After that the boy would be on his own. At NYU he had taken courses in education that would qualify him to teach. At Harvard he could concentrate on literary studies and journalism.

For Countee the summer of waiting and preparation was accompanied by the routine vacation activities. Then came the announcement that awards in the *Crisis*-sponsored competition in literature and art would be presented on the fourteenth of August. The scene was the Renaissance Casino at 138th Street and Seventh Avenue. This building, named in the spirit of the times, was familiar to the young people of Harlem. The first floor housed a movie theater. Upstairs the ballroom had been converted into an auditorium for this special occasion.

The staff of *The Crisis* had exerted every effort to make this contest meaningful to young Negro artists and writers. The names of the judges alone were enough to inspire awe in the contestants. First there was Sinclair Lewis, whose novels *Babbitt, Main Street,* and the Pulitzer Prize–winning *Arrowsmith* were current topics of conversation. Edward Bok, the famous editor and writer, was another judge. The third distinguished critic was Eugene O'Neill, also a Pulitzer Prize winner and America's best known playwright. And W. E. B. DuBois, editor of *The Crisis,* rounded out the list.

The fifteen recipients of awards represented seven states and the District of Columbia. First prize for fiction went to Dr. Rudolph Fisher, then interning at Freedman's Hospital in Washington, D.C. His short story, "High Yaller," depicted the plight of the light-skinned Negro. From Washington also came Willis Richardson, whose "Broken Banjo" placed first in the play division. Marietta Bonner from Massachusetts submitted the winning essay, "On Being Young, a Woman, and Colored." For poetry Countee Cullen received the first place award, thus topping his friends Frank Horne and Langston Hughes (in that order).

Second and third place winners in the various categories were residents of Colorado, New Mexico, Missouri, Ohio, New York, South Carolina, and Indiana. This evidence that the spirit of the Harlem Renaissance was spreading throughout the nation brought joy to the promoters of the contest. The contact with other young minds was stimulating to the contestants. And Cullen was ready to set out for Harvard with another prize in his collection.

In the fall of 1925, Countee arrived in Cambridge to find it a fable come to life. The scull on the Charles River, the ancient trees, the Yard, the clubs, Widener Library, Massachusetts Hall—all invited him to live again in another era. He walked along the campus streets with the friendly ghosts of Emerson, Longfellow, Lowell, Cotton, Mather, Justice Holmes. He could hardly wait to savor the intimacy of places that were as yet only names to him.

One of his earliest discoveries was Houghton Library. The basement of this treasure house abounded in first editions and original manuscripts. Countee was interested to see the works of Emerson, Lowell, Holmes, and Emily Dickinson. But he stared wide-eyed at a first edition of John Keats' first book and at sheets and sheets of poetry in Keats' own handwriting.

Countee found that at Harvard there were many distinctive personalities, too. Robert C. Weaver, then a student of economics and government, became one of his good friends. Even as a student Weaver showed evidences of the ability that led to his later becoming United States Housing Administrator, the first Negro to gain such a high federal position. And among the faculty were men who proved to be friends and counselors as well as professors. Countee's favorite was the noted poet and teacher, Robert Sillman Hillyer.

Two years after his 1917 graduation from Harvard, Hillyer had become an instructor there. Already he had won two of his long string of poetry awards—the Garrison Prize in 1916 and the Verdun Medal in 1917. Countee and his classmates were impressed with the knowledge that their teacher had studied at the University of Copenhagen, that in 1923 he had been named Phi Beta Kappa Poet by the chapter at Tufts University, and that he was now president of the New England Poetry Club.

When Countee enrolled in Mr. Hillyer's course in versification, he anticipated success. After all, he had already had some experience in writing poetry, and he was sure he could learn to do whatever the instructor required. Hillyer believed that poetry was a link between the present and the past. So he taught the techniques of this art by assigning exercises in writing the various traditional forms of English verse. The necessary precision of form and thought made these exercises challenging. Countee went to work on the first assignment with vigor. Then along with his classmates he waited in suspense for the return of the corrected papers, and he was mildly shocked to see the grade of "D" on that first exercise.

On his recovery he was glad to realize that he was about to learn some of the things he really needed to know. Hillyer had faith in Cullen's capabilities and was aware of his desire to learn. So working together they accomplished much and eventually became personal friends. Then when Countee had completed the course he found that eight of his "exercises" were good enough to be included in his next book, *Copper Sun*. In appreciation he dedicated this section of his volume to Robert S. Hillyer.

Years later in a book of his own, Robert Hillyer, who had meanwhile become a Pulitzer Prize winner, paid compliments to his former student by recalling Cullen's classroom work and using one of his poems as an example of poetic form. According to Hillyer, Countee Cullen was the first American poet to publish a poem in rime royal the difficult seven-line stanza made famous by Chaucer and Masefield.

The disappointing mark on Countee's first poetry assignment at Harvard was balanced by a happier experience. On the ninth of December, 1925, *The New York Times* reported the results of the annual Witter Bynner contest. In 1923 and 1924, Cullen's poems had won second place. But this year he was first among college students from all over the country. There had been entries from students at Harvard, Mount Holyoke, Chicago, Cornell, Michigan, and numerous other schools including New York University where Countee was enrolled when he entered the 1925 contest. From the hundreds of poems, the judges—Sara Teasdale, George Sterling, and Witter Bynner himself—had chosen Countee Cullen's verses as the best.

Like most Harvard men Countee found many attractions in the city of Boston, both culturally and socially. By subway, Cambridge was only a few minutes away from the heart of the capital city. When he had the money he could indulge his appetite for lobster or other sea food, or he could enjoy distinctive Yankee menus in the old and famous Durgin-Park restaurant. In Symphony Hall with its fine acoustics Countee satisfied his taste for the best music, thanks to the student rates for tickets.

Music was partly responsible too for his meeting a pretty girl. When Countee was introduced to Sydonia Byrd, she was a student at the New England Conservatory of Music. She had come out of the Middle West—Indianapolis, Indiana, to be exact. Her olive skin and the classic regularity of her features reminded Countee of an Italian painting. And her quiet reserve intrigued him. He found time to visit her frequently, and was finally inspired to address to her fourteen lines of poetry which he called, "Advice to a Beauty." Within the poem he included these lines:

> Beauty beats so frail a wing;
> Suffer men to gaze, poets to sing
> How radiant you are, compare
> And favor you to that most rare
> Bird of delight: a lovely face
> Matched with an equal inner grace.

In this year at Harvard, Countee Cullen found still another facet of life added to his pursuit of learning, of culture, and of social activity. He began to discover that the life of a published author belongs, at least in part, to the public. He was now being invited to appear as a speaker and to give public readings of his poetry.

Even his Christmas vacation was not entirely his own.

On December 30, at the Plaza Hotel in New York, the Reviewers and Critics held a forum on Negro music, poetry, and letters. They had sought popular and competent representatives of these fields to discuss them informally. The selection of speakers was timely. James Weldon Johnson had just published his *Book of American Negro Spirituals,* and the information he gave on the subject was enlivened by the haunting music of these songs. J. Rosamond Johnson (James Weldon's brother) and Taylor Gordon did the singing. The field of letters was represented by Walter White, whose novel *The Fire in the Flint* was a 1925 best seller. Twenty-two-year-old Countee Cullen was deemed competent to handle the subject of poetry by virtue of his having been named winner of the Witter Bynner Prize for 1925.

After the holiday break Cullen went back to Cambridge with a sense of increased responsibility. Although it was pleasant to be acclaimed as a precocious young writer of verse, the words of the critics were sometimes frightening. For example, he read in *Current History* magazine for February, 1926, V. F. Calverton's appraisal of writers represented in Alain Locke's *The New Negro.* Calverton had praised the efforts of Negro artists and writers to portray themselves. Weary of the white authors' unflattering portrayals of colored men and women, they themselves had seized the brush and the pen. Calverton viewed this independence as creative, and he found it good.

He singled out Countee Cullen as the poet who had achieved the most "striking novelty of figure" and the most "infectious beauty of rhythm." The writer went on

60

to say that the best of Cullen's poetry was "abundantly promising, vividly persuasive—a brilliant potential." And the very next month Carl Van Doren had written in *Century* that "the poetry of Countee Cullen is as good as has been written by any American in his teens or early twenties."

Such critical approval reached readers in many places, especially throughout the East. So Countee was not particularly surprised to receive an invitation to read his poetry at the Emerson Hotel in Baltimore. It was the spring of 1926. The letter from the Civic Club had arrived in time for him to plan his schedule with care. Since the lecture was to take place on a Saturday, it would not interfere with his classes.

The early May morning was pleasant as he boarded the train in Boston. In spite of his experience in facing the public, he was always plagued by nervous apprehension, so he welcomed the train ride as an opportunity to collect his thoughts and try to still the butterflies.

He had chosen the selections he planned to read, but there was still time to make changes. So removing from his briefcase his little sheaf of poems he thoughtfully leafed through the pages, pausing here and there to read more carefully. Lately he had found himself writing about love:

> I who employ a poet's tongue
> Would tell you how
> You are a golden damson hung
> Upon a silver bough.

61

He had written these lines as the opening stanza of a poem bemoaning a lover's inability to express his love.

But he was sure that this non-Negro group would expect to hear something on the racial theme. It was not his nature to be overtly militant; he preferred the spiritual approach as revealed in these lines:

> The night whose sable breast relieves the stark,
> White stars is no less lovely being dark. . . .

> So in the dark we hide the heart that bleeds,
> And wait, and tend our agonizing seeds.

As the train approached the Baltimore station, he calmly put his papers in order and started down the aisle. He was ready.

A committee from the Civic Club met him with long faces and embarrassed apologies. The management of the Emerson Hotel had discovered that Mr. Cullen was a Negro. The management regretted that it was against the policy of the hotel to admit a Negro as a guest. The club must remember, the management said, that the hotel had an obligation to its white guests, and after all, this was Maryland.

The delegation from the Civic Club explained to Countee that they had sent him a letter as soon as they learned of the difficulty, but obviously he had left Cambridge before the message was delivered. The best they could do now was to pay him his fee and re-emphasize their apologies. Countee Cullen was nearly speechless. Nevertheless, he managed a few civil remarks. He considered getting in touch with friends in Baltimore. Yolande was now teaching there, and friends and acquaintances of his parents lived there. But there was nothing he could say to them or to anyone at this time. He made his inquiries at the ticket window and boarded the next train to Boston.

Fortunately, Cullen had little time to brood over the humiliating experience. Graduation was only a month away. Examinations and final papers demanded his time and attention. He was also forced to give serious thought to getting a job. The challenge to produce more books was almost overwhelming, especially since he had received such favorable critical comment on *Color*.

There was still another diversion in store for Countee Cullen. It had started back in New York at his father's church. Brother James Canagata was addressing a special meeting of the Official Board. The fervent opening prayer had moved Countee as it had moved all the assembled stewards and trustees. They were excitedly attentive in spite of the fact that they already knew what Brother Canagata was about to tell them—that is, all knew except Pastor Cullen himself.

As the speaker reviewed the twenty-five years of Dr. Cullen's ministry, he could hear softly murmured amens from his brother board members. Brother Canagata could see the look of impatience in Brother Gowins' eyes, but his sense of the dramatic made him work slowly toward the climax. He reminded them of the year 1902 when Frederick Cullen had come to New York to take charge of the struggling mission that was Salem. He described the slow progress that had led to the move to better quarters on 133rd Street in 1912. He spoke of the youth programs and the constantly increasing membership. Then, his voice trembling with pride, he recalled the June day in 1924 when they had joyously moved into this elegant building. And now Dr. Cullen had entered the silver anniversay year of his ministry, and the church was going to celebrate in a way that would not soon be forgotten.

Frederick Cullen shook off the temporary shock to ask himself if what he had just heard could possibly be true. Were they really offering him a trip to the Holy Land? Would he actually walk on the ground where his Lord had trod? When at last he found his voice, the words of gratitude came tumbling out with a force that made these men delighted that they had planned this happy surprise.

But the fact that the offer included passage for Mrs. Cullen called for a family conference. Frederick Cullen knew that Carolyn heartily disliked both ships and water. This trip, however, was the kind of opportunity that might never come again. Perhaps he could convince her.

Carolyn Cullen simply would not hear of it. She reaffirmed her horror at the mere thought of crossing the Atlantic Ocean. Of course, she wanted Pa to take advantage of the church's generous offer, but couldn't he go without her? Alone? She knew the answer before she asked the question. Then suddenly a thought occurred to them so obvious that they had overlooked it at first. Pa need not go alone; Countee could go with him if the Board approved.

The church proved willing, so preparations began. Countee's pulse beat rapidly as he helped work out the itinerary: Le Havre, Paris, Marseille, Alexandria, Beirut, Haifa, Jerusalem, Cairo, Rome, Zurich. They had to apply for passports and visas, sit for photos, and make decisions about clothing and luggage.

Amid these exciting preparations Countee had to keep at least a part of his attention on academic matters, such as completing his graduate work and planning for a career. In 1926, most Negro college graduates entered the traditional professions of law, medicine, and teaching. Writing was not a fruitful occupation for a young man without additional income. Although Countee was eligible for a license to teach, he was afraid that a position in this field would not allow him time to concentrate on his writing. He also had training in journalism, but he had little hope of securing a paying job on the staff of a periodical. He faced a tough decision, and his parents insisted that he himself should be the one to make it.

But this problem was pushed aside momentarily by the arrival of Commencement Day, June 24, 1926. The occasion carried a tremendous emotional impact for Countee as he joined the 1600 candidates for degrees assembling in front of Massachusetts Hall. They formed an aisle of two long lines through which the official dignitaries moved across the Yard, their dark academic gowns accented by colorful hoods and stoles.

This graduation marked the 290th anniversary of the founding of Harvard College. The governor of Massachusetts was there, and uniformed members of the Cavalry and the Lancers added splendor to the pageantry. The ceremonies were held out of doors where stately elms provided shade and the balmy June air kept the crowds comfortable.

After the orations by honor graduates, President Abbott Lawrence Lowell conferred the degrees. Countee Cullen was one of 172 Masters of Arts.

CHAPTER
VI

A<small>T ITS PIER</small> in the Hudson River the *Ile de France* stood
ready for the crossing. There were people everywhere.
Porters threaded their way through the babbling crowds.
Voyagers shouted last-minute messages to their friends.
Some had already gone aboard to make merry at the stateroom bon voyage parties. Even the people who did not
know any of the passengers waved and shouted. They had
come just to join in the excitement that attended the departure of an ocean liner.

The Cullens, making their way through the gaiety and
confusion, had little opportunity for an organized assess-
ment of their situation. Yet, somehow, they were aware of
the uniqueness of their position. In 1926, it was still unusual for Negroes to travel abroad. Those who were fortunate enough to go acquired a degree of prestige and were
looked upon with envy by their friends and acquaintances.
So Frederick Cullen humbly realized that he had come a

long way from the barefoot days in Maryland to the luxury of this floating palace.

Like all novice sailors Countee was fascinated by the
ship. He was a little boy again, testing the beds in the
stateroom, rushing out to find the deck chair that matched
the number on his coupon, inspecting the shuffleboard
markings, getting lost in the maze of corridors and salons.
There was not much sleeping the first night out. Indeed
Countee, who after five years of college study had become
a night person, considered it a shame to waste any time
in sleep during the entire trip.

The lifeboat drill was an interesting experience. It was
easy to spot the first-time travelers. They assembled
promptly on signal, clutching their instruction sheets and
wearing sober countenances. The experienced travelers
were more casual and had to be prodded by the politely
insistent sailors to find their stations and try on the life
jackets. But Countee soon found that the French Line did
not intend to let its passengers have much time to worry
about possible disasters. Much of the time was spent consuming the five meals a day—continental breakfast, mid-
morning snack, luncheon, afternoon tea, and dinner.

Ma would have found the food a challenge to her own
cooking skills. Even the elaborate menus printed in
French did not fully prepare the diner for the tantalizing
dishes. The tight-jacketed garçons served deftly and cour-
teously. Each night the dinner entree immediately became Countee's favorite; the orange-flavored duck surpassed the lobster, and the succulent lamb surpassed the
duck. Afternoon tea on deck was another delightful and

fattening experience, for the pastry chef outdid himself each day with new varieties of cakes artfully decorated with fluffy butter cream.

The Cullens had friends on board. Dr. Alain Locke, was on his way to Europe and was readily available for good conversation and travel advice. With his serious eyes set deep in a lean, brown face he impressed his acquaintances as a kindly, quiet, and brilliant man. Miss Dorothy Peterson, an attractive Negro teacher from Brooklyn, was a lively addition to the circle. And Arthur Fauset, the Negro folklore specialist and writer, rounded out the group.

Countee found that these people added considerably to his enjoyment of the voyage. And by the time they approached Le Havre, the gang had cooked up an idea. Since the ship was to dock after midnight, the passengers would not disembark until a decent hour in the morning. But word had leaked out that for a price the head steward would let you go ashore and spend a few hours in the city before taking the boat train to Paris. Countee and his friends were quick to grasp this opportunity.

So in the early morning on the ninth of July, 1926, Countee Cullen walked for the first time on foreign soil. His companions were experienced travelers. Alain Locke had studied in England, Dorothy Peterson had grown up in Puerto Rico, and Arthur Fauset had done research in Nova Scotia. But they did not deflate Countee's naïve exuberance with their sophistication. Pa had remained on the ship, so the adventurers were free to explore the streets and cafés and to mingle with the people in this seaport town. Countee strained his ears to unravel the rapid sounds of a language that bore little resemblance to classroom French.

The hours flew by and they had to hurry to get back to the ship, find Dr. Cullen, and get their luggage onto the boat train. When at last they were settled in their seats, young Cullen divided his attention between the fascinating compartment and the neat patches of farm land that raced past the window. They were on their way to Paris. He kept telling his father that they must make every minute count. There was much to see and so little time. Pa was sympathetic to his son's feeling of urgency.

Arriving in Paris on a midsummer afternoon, the Cullens were duly impressed. They hurried to get settled in their hotel rooms, for they were eager to go out and explore the city. That very evening with some of their shipboard friends they rode down the Champs Elysées and through the Bois de Boulogne. Their two brief days became a glorious fusion of all the famous landmarks of the beautiful French capital.

Even in so short a time they discovered how warm and helpful Parisians could be. And they learned to rely on the office of the American Express as an information center and a place to meet Negro Americans abroad. Here they ran into Mercer Cook and his wife. Cook, an expert in the French language, was an Amherst graduate and the son of a famed musician, Will Marion Cook, and his actress wife, Abbie Mitchell. Seeing them here was a welcome reminder of home for the Cullens even though they entertained no thoughts of being homesick. They were kept busy attending Sunday Mass at the Madeleine, exploring

70

the artists' colony in Montmartre, climbing the hill to the white-domed Sacré-Coeur, and sipping coffee or brandy at the sidewalk cafés. Too soon they found themselves at the Gare de Lyons waiting for the morning train to Marseille, their point of embarkation for Alexandria.

Countee was not prepared for the Mediterranean Sea. He was dazzled by its blueness. He wanted to find words to describe the color but could not. From the deck of the Syrian ship he looked away out over the water, squinting against the glare, heedless of the excitement around him. They were passing the place where the whale had swallowed Jonah, and his dad was reliving Biblical times; but Countee was composing a poem.

He found a quiet place to put down the thoughts in his neat handwriting. "Not Helen's eyes," he wrote, . . . "not those proud fans the peacocks spread" . . . "no sky wore such a hue."

> Only the hand that never erred
> Bent on beauty, creation-spurred,
> Could mix and mingle such a dye,
> Nor leave its like in earth or sky.

Everywhere there was poetry. Countee could sense it on the riotous dock at Alexandria, in the library of Alexander the Great, in the dirt and poverty of Beirut, in the giddying drive to Haifa far above the Mediterranean.

Sitting beside his father in a very old motorcar Countee felt all the maturity of his twenty-three years as he tried to still Pa's growing uneasiness. In the dark of the night their daredevil driver rounded curves at a hair-raising

71

speed in the endless climb to Jerusalem. Finally on the distant hills they saw the lights of the city. The sight gave them some comfort; but Pa could not withhold a prayer of thanks when at midnight they reached their hotel.

The next morning both father and son were inspired by the sight of Jerusalem in daylight. Pa was moved by the traditional attractions: the Church of the Holy Sepulchre, Mt. Calvary, the ascension stone, the Church of Simon the Cyrenian, the Via Dolorosa, the Garden of Gethsemane. Countee saw the city in a different light. He wrote:

> A city builded on a hill may flaunt
> Its glory in the sunken valley's face,
> And ways the Nazarene had trod may vaunt
> A credible inheritance of grace.
> Your very stones, Jerusalem, can sing:
> 'He would have taken us beneath his wing.'

From Jerusalem they went through the Suez Canal and then across the Sahara Desert to Cairo. There with other tourists in the museum they gawked at the fabulous King Tut in his solid gold coffin. On another day the Cullens mounted camels for an unsteady ride to the Pyramids and the Sphinx. Later they jostled their way through the bazaars, respectfully removed their shoes to enter the mosques, visited more tombs, then sailed up the Nile past Pharaoh's palace and on to the Red Sea.

By the first of August they were on their way to Rome. They were getting to be experienced travelers now, the father erect, spare, and dignified, the son shorter, lively, and curious. They were amazed at the number of paintings and statues and crumbling ruins and fountains and churches they could see in three days. At night the older man would not go to bed without writing in his diary a careful notation of the day's experiences. Sometimes he would call out to Countee for verification.

On their last day in Rome they went to the Protestant Cemetery. There Countee stood bareheaded before the Shelley memorial and read the familiar inscription, *Cor Cordium*, heart of hearts. These words, he decided, would be the title of his poem. It would be his personal tribute to the impatient young poet who was drowned at the age of thirty. Naturally Countee's thoughts turned to the beautiful lines of "Adonais," the elegy that Shelley had written on the death of Keats. And he remembered, too, the ode in which Shelley had expressed his longing to be a lyre on which the West Wind might play its tumultuous song.

But it was at the century-old grave of John Keats that Countee found his sense of empathy almost overpowering. This tryst was the climax of years of admiration. And Keats' familiar lyrics now raced through Cullen's mind. Images from the Grecian urn, the song of the nightingale, lines from "La Belle Dame Sans Merci," all vied for places in his memory. He reflected that he himself was now only three years younger than Keats had been when he died. Now he, Countee Cullen, was actually reading on the tomb the epitaph Keats himself had chosen: "Here lies one whose name was writ in water."

Countee recalled having read some of the unfavorable

criticisms of Keats' first major work, "Endymion," based
on a story from mythology of the young sun, Endymion,
and his love for Diana, the moon goddess. Countee had
been touched by the romantic beauty of the poem and resented the criticism. At the cemetery he began to plan the
sonnet he would write to commemorate his visit. He called
it, "To Endymion," and closed with these lines:

> High as the star of that last poignant cry
> Death could not stifle in the wasted frame,
> You know at length the bright immortal lie
> Time gives to those detractors of your name,
> And see, from where you and Diana ride,
> Your humble epitaph—how misapplied.

Although the visit in Rome was followed by a few days
among the natural wonders of Switzerland, Countee could
not immediately shake off the effects of his emotional experience at the Protestant Cemetery. But the return to
Paris was therapeutic. Now he had two weeks to explore
the "City of Light." He loved the beauty and gaiety of
the boulevards and the sidewalk cafés. He soon learned
the places that served the best onion soup, and he quickly
acquired the habit of stopping in for this delicacy after an
evening's entertainment.

One night the Cullens taxied to the Place Boieldieu and
entered the Opera Comique. The building was young by
European standards, just twenty-eight years old. But it
was older in tradition. It had been destroyed by fire in
1887. Eleven years later the music-loving Parisians had
rebuilt the theater on the same site. An usherette escorted
the Cullens to their seats. Countee had been told of the

customary tipping in French theaters, so he fumbled in his pocket for the necessary centimes. He was rewarded with two programs, and he and his father settled back in their plush-lined seats to enjoy a memorable evening.

They were not to be disappointed. The double bill included *Tosca* and *Cavalleria Rusticana*. When the curtain went up on *Tosca*, Countee shivered in anticipation. He had never before seen an opera where some of the lines were actually spoken instead of being sung. And although this was not a happy story, what with its several murders and suicides, the highly dramatic moments made it exciting.

From the very start of *Cavalleria Rusticana*, Countee began to concentrate on Mascagni's music, listening for the strains that were familiar to him. Pa was immediately impressed by the Easter music in the opening scene. But for Countee the great moment arrived as the orchestra with harps and organ played the beautiful intermezzo. And despite the gruesome ending he found himself humming the melody of the intermezzo along with the rest of the audience as they left the theater.

There was not time to do half the things they had planned nor to go to the many places that had been recommended by friends. Their token visit to the Louvre aroused the ambition to return to Paris and spend long hours before their favorite paintings. They had only fleeting moments to look at Notre Dame, the Eiffel Tower, and the Pantheon. They hurried through the luxurious Palace of Fontainebleau. By the end of August it was time to leave for Le Havre and begin their journey home.

The Cullens were glad to have the companionship of

Dr. Locke again on the return voyage. To their further delight Arthur Schomberg had also booked passage on this ship. This author of several books and historical pamphlets was already gaining a reputation as a book collector. The four men, the only Negroes on board, made an agreeable party, since both Schomberg and Countee had been contributors to Locke's recent book, *The New Negro*.

On their fifth day at sea the liner ran into a severe storm. Countee could hardly believe that such a large vessel could be tossed so mercilessly by the rolling sea. Passengers began to wonder whether the ship would turn over as it mounted the huge waves or sink under the tons of water that poured onto the decks. Finally some of the passengers, having discovered that Dr. Cullen was a minister, asked him to lead them in prayer. A large number of people followed him into a salon where he conducted an impromptu service. He prayed fervently, talked calmly, and led his audience in singing familiar hymns. Soon thereafter the storm subsided, and the journey continued without incident. The only real inconvenience was a late arrival in New York.

The Cullens came home to fair and mild weather that made Countee feel fresh and eager. He wanted to get home and see Ma. He also wondered about his writing friends. He was anxious to compare notes with them on their plans for the great novels, plays, and poems they hoped to produce. Fortunately, he could expect to be right in the center of Harlem's artistic life. In a few weeks he was going to work on the editorial staff of *Opportunity* magazine for the Urban League.

76

CHAPTER
VII

W<small>HEN</small> <small>AUTUMN</small> <small>DESCENDED</small> on New York in 1926, Countee Cullen felt the emptiness that usually comes in September to recent college graduates. For the first time in seventeen years he would not be going to school. Now he faced the problem of earning a living. Although he was serious about his work as a poet, he was enough of a realist to know that he could not expect to live on his poetry.

There were men at the Urban League who realized this too. Even while he was a college student Countee had earned the respect of Charles Spurgeon Johnson, editor of *Opportunity*. Cullen had been a winner in the 1925 *Opportunity* literary contest, and Mr. Johnson had been following his career with interest. He believed that Countee belonged on the magazine, so he made him assistant editor.

On the first of October, Countee stood before the glass doors where black lettering identified the offices of the National Urban League. He entered the small reception room and passed through the wooden swinging gate that separated visitors from employees. The most important office belonged to Eugene Kinckle Jones, the wiry, energetic executive secretary of the organization. Additional offices were occupied by other men who carried on the business and research projects of the League.

As its name implies, this organization was concerned with problems confronting Negroes in urban areas. After the first World War there was an influx of Negroes from the rural South to the cities of the North. The resulting problems were numerous and alarming. They encompassed the fields of housing, employment, education, race relations, and adjustment to an entire new way of living. The League undertook many surveys to determine the nature of the difficulties faced by new residents and to find ways of resolving them. Dedicated personnel worked with business firms and individuals to find suitable employment for colored workers. Leaders of industry and representatives of the trade unions accepted positions on the organization's most important councils and committees.

In the Urban League offices, Charles Johnson presided over the area allotted to *Opportunity*. Countee's respect for his chief was founded on more than their compatible personalities. The older man was an outstanding scholar and sociologist. For several years in his quiet way he had sought to interpret and improve the plight of the Negro. And now in recent years he had founded a magazine, at first to record and publicize the League's economic progress. But lately he had become concerned with the welfare of young writers.

Slim and neat, and looking like a young college professor in his mahogany chair, Johnson explained his policy to his young assistant. He wanted to make the magazine's pages available for the manuscripts of talented unknown Negroes. But more than this, he wanted to open opportunities for acceptance of their works by more prominent publications. He hoped to rely on Countee's literary background for the screening of manuscripts and for editorial suggestions.

Mr. Johnson adjusted his metal-rimmed spectacles and proceeded to elaborate on plans for the assistant editor. In addition to reading copy, Cullen was to have his own column. Here he could review new books and comment generally on the literary scene.

The column, which Countee decided to call "The Dark Tower," made its debut in December with an enthusiastic review of Elizabeth Madox Roberts' *The Time of Man*. In a later column he reviewed *In Abraham's Bosom, Porgy,* and *Black Velvet,* all current Broadway productions involving the Negro. Sometimes he discussed poetry, and in one column he introduced some poems by Lula Lowe Weeden, an eight-year-old girl who dictated her lyrical descriptions to her mother.

A strikingly poignant edition of "The Dark Tower" appeared when the column was a year old. The Negro community had just lost two young women of widely different talents and backgrounds. One was Clarissa Scott Delany, a writer and teacher. She was a Wellesley graduate, the daughter of Howard University's treasurer, Emmett Jay Scott, and bride of a young lawyer from a highly respected

79

and successful family. The other was Florence Mills, the beautiful little dancing star of the popular musical, *Blackbirds*. In his tribute Cullen said in part:

Death the terrible, that comes like a thief in the night or, if he wills to linger, with the stealthy but certain slowness of a malignant disease; Death, the irreverent disrespector of persons, sparing neither maid nor matron, celebrity nor nonentity; Death the capricious, who takes the bride in the midst of her nuptial blushes and the dancer on her most applauded pirouette, in making them our common bereavement has drawn them into a juxtaposition life never suffered them to know.

And later in the same column, speaking of Florence Mills he wrote:

There was about her none of that raucous air that membership in the Methodist Church has taught us to expect of actresses. . . . We have silenced many a puritan lady, her mind and senses as laced and buttoned as her outmoded garments, by querying when she spoke, out of her cloistered ignorance, of the terrible obscenity of the Negro stage: 'But have you seen Florence Mills?'

Charles Johnson's vision of his magazine's role in promoting Negro writers was fulfilled in great measure. The results of the Opportunity Literary Contests had been heartening. Entries poured in from ambitious writers in many states. Most of them had prepared themselves in the best schools they could afford, and all seemed eager to carve a new role for the Negro in American culture.

In the 1925 contest the short story division with a top prize of a hundred dollars had disclosed among its winning manuscripts a story by John Matheus. He was a native of West Virginia who taught romance languages in a Negro college in his home state. In this same category was a story by Zora Neale Hurston, a Floridian who had come to New York for a career in journalism. She later became secretary to the novelist Fannie Hurst and went on to study anthropology at Columbia. In third place was Eric Walrond, a product of British Guiana. Walrond had already begun a literary career by contributing to *Vanity Fair, The New Republic,* and *Saturday Review,* and had become business manager of *Opportunity* by the time Cullen joined the staff.

In this same contest the poetry division had been dominated by Langston Hughes and Countee Cullen. Hughes, then living in Washington, D.C., had won first prize with "The Weary Blues," Cullen had received second prize, and they had tied for third place. The judges decided to divide the third prize between Clarissa Scott of Washington and Joseph S. Cotter of Louisville, Kentucky.

There were awards for essays, too. E. Franklin Frazier, a sociologist, had won first prize in this category for an essay on "Social Equality." Frazier had become Director of the Atlantic School for Social Work after several years of experience and study climaxed by a year abroad as an American Scandinavian Fellow. Sterling Brown, another essayist, who was later to be heard from in the field of poetry, won second prize. His offering was a tribute to Roland Hayes, the Negro tenor whose voice had thrilled audiences in concert halls all over the world. Brown had been a Phi Beta Kappa student at Williams College, and with a master's degree from Harvard was currently engaged in teaching. The third place winner in this division, Laura D. Wheatley of Baltimore, had chosen to write about "The Negro Poet."

Other writers in the vanguard of the Negro Renaissance were early contributors to *Opportunity* although they had not entered the contests. Among them were Claude McKay and Jean Toomer. For Countee, contact with all of these people was one of the most rewarding aspects of his job.

He had known some of them before he came to this position. He remembered particularly his early acquaintance with Arna Bontemps. This young man had come from California while Cullen was still a student at NYU. Langston Hughes once described Bontemps as "quiet and scholarly, looking like a young edition of Dr. Dubois." Countee, never averse to making new friends, was happy to find someone with literary interests akin to his own.

Shortly after Bontemps' arrival in New York, Countee was invited to a dance at the Renaissance Casino. He thought this would be a good occasion for a newcomer to meet people and dispel the loneliness that often affects strangers in a big city. So he invited his new friend. At first Bontemps was hesitant to accept the invitation because he didn't know a girl in town to invite. But Countee had an answer. He was taking Yolande, of course, and he was sure he could arrange for Bontemps to date one of his favorite cousins, Roberta Bosley.

The Renaissance Casino was new and attractive and a favorite place of recreation for young Harlemites. Here the devotees of the Charleston and the Big Apple displayed their dancing talents to the music of the jazz bands that were in vogue at the time. Countee's dancing skill was the envy of his friends. Some of them maintained that the rhythm left over from his poetry went to his feet. At any rate he thoroughly enjoyed the music, and he and his friends had a jolly time.

While Countee was working at *Opportunity*, the Negro writers recruited by Charles Johnson and others began to enjoy an unprecedented amount of publicity. Help came from a number of sources. But among the promoters of Negro arts and letters perhaps the most interesting was a Negro woman. Mrs. A'Leilia Walker Robinson was an heiress. Her mother, Madam C. J. Walker, had made a fortune by inventing a method of straightening hair. The daughter owned, among other properties, a house on 136th Street where she welcomed writers, painters, sculptors, musicians, and people interested in the arts. She provided a vivid background for these meetings. In one room there was a grand piano painted gold. Another room, decorated in black and red and gold, featured on the wall two poems: "The Weary Blues" by Langston Hughes, and "From the Dark Tower" by Countee Cullen. This room became popularly known as The Dark Tower.

A'Leilia Walker was a lavish entertainer, and Countee was among the inner core of writers who were invited to all her parties. They were usually crowded because she wanted to give aspiring artists a chance to meet people who could help them. So she gathered in every agent, producer, and publisher she could reach. And in addition she

83

sought out wealthy men and women with the hope that they would become patrons of her young friends.

A familiar figure at these gatherings was Carl Van Vechten. He could usually be seen at the foot of the stairs that led to the salons on an upper floor. There he stood resting an elbow on a convenient newel post and affably greeting all comers without the trouble of battling the crowds to find the persons he wanted to see.

Countee could usually find his friends here—Arna Bontemps and Langston Hughes, of course, and Harold Jackman. Harold, though not a writer, had a keen interest in literature and the theater. He had been born in London and educated in two of the same schools that Countee later attended, De Witt Clinton High and NYU. Jackman was now a teacher. He was one of the friends with whom Countee enjoyed discussing literature, for Harold had made himself an authority on the Negro in the arts. In addition he was an excellent bridge partner.

Any guest looking for variety could find it at one of A'Leilia's parties. Philanthropists rubbed shoulders with such people as Florence Mills, band leader Jimmy Lunceford, and singer-actor Paul Robeson. James Weldon Johnson or Walter White might be seen in conversation not only with serious students of sociology but also with eccentric whites looking for a novel way to spend an evening.

There was always a tempting buffet with plenty to eat and drink. But getting to it required some dexterity. A'Leilia always invited more people than the place could possibly hold. This strategy gave those who did get in a feeling of accomplishment. So her parties became increasingly popular.

On Saturdays during the summer, The Dark Tower was available to visiting and native college students for tea dances. College students on vacation provided the music just for the joy of playing. Here the younger set made friends and encouraged each other in working toward careers in the arts.

The Dark Tower parties were duplicated on a less lavish scale by other Harlem hosts and hostesses. All the affairs were not as cosmopolitan as A'Leilia's, but they served the purpose of promoting the arts. Mrs. Lillian Alexander usually entertained a more conservative group. She and her husband, Dr. Ernest Alexander, a successful dermatologist, lived in a tastefully furnished home on a street known to Harlemites as "Striver's Row." This block of houses on 139th Street between Seventh and Eighth avenues had been designed by the well-known architect, Stanford White. The Negroes who bought them took such pride in their upkeep that it was a pleasure to walk along the quiet street where a row of trees gently shaded the light brick houses with their beautifully curtained windows.

Mrs. Alexander, affectionately known to her friends as "Sally," was a social leader. She had traveled in Europe and had a wide circle of friends. One room in her home was furnished with articles she had acquired in her travels and an assortment of old pieces she could not bear to discard. She laughingly referred to this room as her British Museum.

At her parties Sally made sure that the "old guard" intellectuals did not take a back seat to the less conservative artists. She had little regard for sensationalism, and she was rather skeptical of the indiscriminate publicity given to works that pictured the Negro as exotic or primitive. She was equally discriminating in choosing her white guests, shunning thrill-seekers and do-gooders alike.

The James Weldon Johnsons' parties had an intellectual flavor, too. Mr. Johnson's appearance and background did not inspire levity. He was tall, lean, and immaculate. The younger people who met him were awed by his versatility and the variety of his accomplishments. He had a law degree and had taught school. He had written librettos for opera and songs for musical comedy. For seven years he had been a United States Consul in Central and South America. He spoke fluent Spanish. His writing credits were numerous. He had been awarded the Spingarn Medal. And now he was executive secretary of the NAACP. But as a host he was modest and self-effacing, always focusing attention on others. And in the well-appointed home that exuded culture and comfort the Johnsons' guests could generally count on meeting interesting personalities such as Van Vechten or Clarence Darrow.

Such entertainment was not confined to Harlem, however. In the twenties, parties were not uncommon in Greenwich Village where artists and pseudo-artists were interested in cultivating the "new Negro." An occasional host in the village was Colonel Arthur Spingarn, a sup-

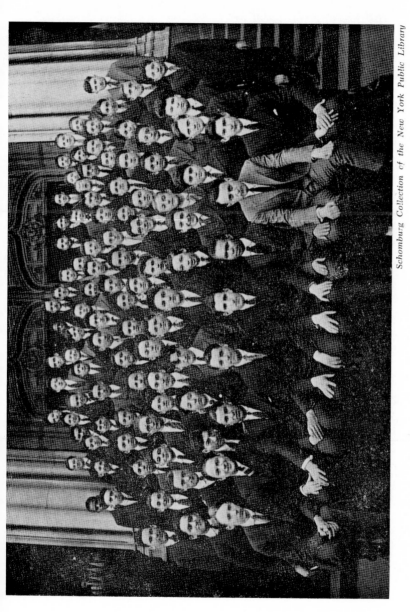

The Class of 1922, from the De Witt Clinton High School Yearbook of 1921.
(Countee Cullen seated in front row.)

Lenox Avenue at 135th Street in the 1930's

Countee Cullen, a pastel portrait by Winold Reiss

William Edward Burghardt Du Bois

Alain Locke

Countee Cullen in 1939

James Weldon Johnson, reproduced from a portrait by
Laura Wheeler Waring

Countee Cullen in 1941, photographed by Carl Van Vechten

porter of the NAACP and donor of the Spingarn Medal for Negro achievement.

But the most exciting gatherings outside of Harlem were those at the home of Carl Van Vechten and his charming wife, the former Fania Marinoff. Visitors entered a spacious book-lined hall. This and other rooms of the apartment were dominated by literally thousands of books. And the walls of the large, cheerful living room were alive with original paintings by contemporary artists, both white and Negro. Here sometimes the aspiring writers were fortunate enough to meet Witter Bynner or Fannie Hurst, or perhaps Hugh Walpole or Somerset Maugham. Everyone felt comfortable here, for Van Vechten, who dressed informally for these occasions, was a delightful host.

Of course, the interracial relations resulting from the newly awakened interest in the Negro did not always promote the arts. The Harlem nightclubs were a case in point. Drawn by the musical talents of entertainers like Duke Ellington and lesser known jazz artists, white New Yorkers and visitors flocked to the Negro cabarets. These spots were now a "must" on their sightseeing lists. Eventually this practice backfired as Negro proprietors, eager to encourage white patronage, began to exclude their colored customers. As a result there was little difference between Harlem night spots and those downtown except, perhaps, for the Negro performers on stage.

But the white cafe-goers wanted more than a stage performance. This they could get in the Broadway theaters where shows like *Shuffle Along* and *Blackbirds* offered the finest in Negro dancing, singing, and band playing, and where Bill "Bojangles" Robinson, Ethel Waters, and Florence Mills were the stars of the day. Nightclub patrons expected to see and mingle with Harlemites on a more intimate basis, and this experience was denied them when they were the only guests.

The private soirees, however, were more discriminating and thus more successful in establishing personal contacts. In ever increasing numbers New Yorkers and other Americans were becoming aware of the Negro's creative efforts.

One of the first benefactors to recognize these efforts was the wealthy philanthropist William E. Harmon. In December, 1926, the first awards of the Harmon Foundation were announced. In fine arts the prize went to Palmer Hayden; James C. Evans won in science, Max Yergan in religion, C. C. Spaulding in business, and Will W. Alexander (a white Southerner) in race relations. The five-hundred-dollar first award in literature was given to Countee Cullen, the youngest winner, for his first book of poetry, *Color*.

CHAPTER
VIII

THE SHARP DECEMBER WIND cut through his topcoat as Countee rang the doorbell at the DuBois home. It was Christmas eve. He felt in his pocket for the little jewel box and his fingers trembled as he touched it. Inside the house he asked immediately to see Dr. DuBois. He came frankly to the point. He wanted Yolande to accept his engagement ring, and he needed her father's blessing.

Countee knew he was not the only suitor. But he felt that his education, his sincerity as a writer, and his respectable job qualified him as a competitor. Knowing the closeness between Yolande and her father he assumed that the older man's opinion would have some influence. Dr. DuBois, however, was friendly but noncommittal. Indeed he had discussed with Yolande all the young men, their qualifications and their family backgrounds. But to Countee he merely said that Yolande herself would have to make the decision. Fortunately his daughter accepted Countee promptly with no display of maidenly coyness.

The holiday season sparkled with the joy of celebrating their engagement. When the festivities were over, the self-discipline that Countee had acquired early in life served him well, for he was producing two books in addition to doing his work on the magazine. The first of these books was *Copper Sun*, his second volume of verse, dedicated to Yolande. In this volume he included his special poem for her, "One Day We Played a Game." These idyllic lines pictured the young couple under an apple tree. They made a game of recalling famous pairs of lovers from Heloise and Abelard to Adam and Eve.

Countee divided the book into five sections. The first part, called "Color," dealt with the emotions he felt as a Negro. He began with a ray of hope that promised:

> We shall not always plant while others reap
> The golden increment of bursting fruit, . . .

and he dedicated the poem, titled "From the Dark Tower," to Charles S. Johnson. Other verses portrayed vivid images—a colored blues singer, a proud black girl in her new red hat, a brown girl lovely and victorious in death.

The second section of *Copper Sun* bore the caption "The Deep in Love." Here the first poem, "Pity the Deep in Love," was inscribed to Fiona Braithwaite. This young Bostonian was the daughter of William Stanley Braithwaite, himself a poet, but better known as editor of seventeen volumes of an anthology of American poetry spanning the years 1913 to 1929. Although his poem to Yolande dominated the love section in *Copper Sun*, other lyrics harped on the themes of unrequited love and faithless sweethearts.

The eight poems written in Mr. Hillyer's class formed the third part of the volume. They were labeled simply "At Cambridge," and included the English verse forms that Cullen had learned to execute with competence. The section ended with "To Lovers of Earth, Fair Warning," the poem in rime royal that Hillyer later praised and quoted in his book.

There followed a variety of poems in Part Four titled "Varia." Here Cullen placed the four pieces he had composed during that memorable journey abroad with his father—the tributes to Shelley and Keats and his reactions to the city of Jerusalem and its Wailing Wall. Here too were his "Lines to My Father." There was also a stanza dedicated to Amy Lowell and one to John Haynes Holmes written for the Twentieth Anniversay Dinner given by a grateful community in honor of the celebrated preacher. (Dr. Holmes later wrote a touching letter of appreciation, saying the poem was "characteristic of your genius and moved me greatly.")

Copper Sun ended with a group of seven poems under the caption "Juvenilia." These were products of Cullen's youth, some of them written during his high school days at Clinton.

Critical reaction to this volume, while generally favorable, did not measure up to that burst of acclaim that had greeted his first book, *Color*. But Countee was encouraged to read among the reviews a statement in *The Nation* that said in part, "Best of all he can forget that he is of the colored race and be just 'poet' most of the time."

Later in 1927, Harper and Brothers published *Caroling Dusk,* an anthology of verse by Negro poets, edited by Countee Cullen. This book was one of Cullen's most important contributions to the Negro Renaissance. Through his position on the staff of the magazine he came to know most of the young poets who had been discovered in the past few years. Many of them had been published in *The Crisis* and *Opportunity.* Some had won literary contests. Certain ones kept in constant touch with Countee, asking for criticism of their work.

In his foreword to *Caroling Dusk* Cullen frankly stated that his primary purpose was to present these new voices to the reading public. But he included the work of established poets too, and in all there were selections by thirty-eight Negroes, ranging chronologically from Paul Laurence Dunbar to eight-year-old Lula Lowe Weeden.

Selecting the poems for the anthology was difficult. Countee anticipated criticism because he believed there was no such thing as Negro poetry. He pointedly designated his selections "verse by Negro poets." Already he had contributed to a symposium in *The Crisis* an article defending his view that Negro authors should not be bound to respect the "implied conditions" of publishers restricting them to racial material. So he tried to include in *Caroling Dusk* poems with subject matter that was not essentially Negroid. His critics contended that his point was at best theoretical, since Cullen himself admitted that there were certain experiences, such as racial injustices, peculiar to Negro life.

The anthology began with eight poems by Dunbar, who, according to Cullen, was the first Negro to achieve a place of distinction as an American poet. Since his work was primarily done in the late nineteenth century (he died in 1906), Dunbar might be considered a forerunner of the Renaissance writers. Cullen included in the book only one of the dialect poems for which Dunbar had been so famous. Only one poem of the remaining seven, "We Wear the Mask," dealt with the anguish of the Negro, and even here Dunbar did not in so many words identify the "we" as Negroes.

James Weldon Johnson, another contributor to the anthology, had begun to write before many of the younger poets were born. And by the time *Caroling Dusk* was published, he had already made considerable progress in a varied and distinguished career. Born in Florida he had moved to New York at the beginning of the century. With the great metropolis as his base of operation he had written lyrics for light opera, served as United States Consul in Venezuela and Nicaragua, translated a Spanish libretto for the Metropolitan Opera Company, and worked as a prize-winning editor of a Negro weekly newspaper. The vitality of New York, his adopted city, had inspired him to write "My City," one of the poems he contributed to Cullen's anthology.

Johnson's devotion to the welfare of the black man had been long and tireless. Since the time when he had accompanied the elder Cullen to Washington on behalf of the

Negro soldiers involved in the Houston trouble, he had been continuously active in the NAACP. He represented the Association in an investigation of misrule in Haiti, and he later became executive secretary of the organization.

In several of his published works Johnson showed his concern for the recognition of the Negro's contribution to American arts and literature. He wrote *The Book of American Negro Poetry, The Book of American Negro Spirituals,* a *Second Book of Negro Spirituals,* and *God's Trombones (Seven Negro Sermons in Verse).* From the latter book "The Creation" was selected for inclusion in *Caroling Dusk.* This version of the story from *Genesis* written in the spirit of the typical Negro preacher was widely acclaimed for the richness of its imagery and the homely tenderness of its language.

DuBois was another forerunner of the Renaissance. When *Caroling Dusk* was published he was editor of *The Crisis.* But much earlier, in 1906, he had written "A Litany of Atlanta," the poem by which he was represented in Cullen's collection. In these lines strong with the flavor of the Old Testament, DuBois made a powerful outcry against the injustices of the white man that led to the Atlanta massacre, an event he had witnessed when he was a college professor in that city.

Equally as outspoken as DuBois was Claude McKay, the bitter young man from the West Indies. Born in Jamaica he had received his early education there and at the age of twenty had published his first book, *Songs of Jamaica.* In the United States he attended college for two years and then began to concentrate on writing and foreign travel. He later placed poems in several magazines, and in 1922 his popular book, *Harlem Shadows*, appeared. From this volume came five of the eight poems he contributed to *Caroling Dusk*.

Langston Hughes was also a published poet before Cullen compiled the anthology, having produced *The Weary Blues* and *Fine Clothes to the Jew*. His was a dominant voice of the Renaissance with particular emphasis on the importance of the Negro masses. His original treatment of the "blues" rhythms lent his poems a folklike quality, and his themes also appealed to the common man. Several of his poems in *Caroling Dusk* have had continuing popularity. Through the years on many a church or school program Negro boys and girls have recited "I Too," "The Negro Speaks of Rivers," and "Mother to Son."

From his own poems Cullen chose the one that had started him on his career, "I Have a Rendezvous with Life." He also included one about Keats and the rime royal poem. These were all nonracial. But interestingly enough he selected a greater number of poems dealing with race. Notable among them was one called "Incident," about an eight-year-old who smiled at a white boy in Baltimore, only to be called "Nigger" in return. In his set of "Four Epitaphs," one was inscribed to his grandmother and another to Keats, but the third was for Paul Laurence Dunbar and the last the well-known epitaph for the lady who expected black cherubs to do her chores in heaven. He chose also "From the Dark Tower" and "Yet Do I Marvel," a poem whose last lines were to be widely quoted on the fly leaves of other authors' books and, in one case, as a book title (*To Make a Poet Black*):

> Yet do I marvel at this curious thing:
> To make a poet black and bid him sing!

Most of the readers of *Caroling Dusk* were seeing the poetry of Arna Bontemps for the first time. This young teacher had recently come to New York from Los Angeles and was to prove himself a versatile and scholarly writer —novelist, essayist, biographer. His eleven poems in the anthology were marked by a gentle, almost mystic quality, their themes embracing nature, race, and religion.

Another young and unpublished poet, Gwendolyn Bennett, had been Cullen's predecessor at *Opportunity*. She had worked there as Mr. Johnson's assistant during the summer of 1926 after returning from a year in France as an art student on scholarship. Her feeling for color and form was evident in the ten selections she contributed to the anthology.

Running through the verses of the newer poets there seemed to be a desire to convince the Negro of his own worth, his unique beauty, and his dignity, and to impress this picture on the minds of other readers. Such was the aim of Gladys Hayford, born on the African Gold Coast, educated in England, and determined to extol the beauty of her homeland and its people. In a similar vein Edward S. Silvera, then a junior in college, wrote of the jungle beauty inherent in the faces of black women and in the songs of Negro Americans. And Helene Johnson, a Bostonian studying in New York, could see the grace of African rhythms reflected in a Harlem street dancer.

Lula Lowe Weeden, aged eight, was the youngest contributor to *Caroling Dusk*. Her poems, sent by her mother from their home in Lynchburg, Virginia, were completely devoid of race consciousness. Lula was concerned with the wonders she kept discovering around her—the moon and stars sticking together, the stream running to meet the Atlantic, and the baldheaded dandelion.

The role of *Caroling Dusk* in helping Negroes to gain recognition in the arts was significant. Although the book was devoted exclusively to poetry, many of the poets represented in it were also writing fiction, painting pictures, and making music. It must be said also that there was not complete agreement as to what the goal of the new Negroes should be. Some believed that they should be militant now that they had the public ear. Others accused their fellow writers of writing what the white reader expected in order to assure themselves of publication. Some said that Cullen slavishly followed white tradition, although most critics agreed he found fresh and highly personal ways of using these old forms. But one thing stood out clearly. The new Negro had abandoned the old tradition of bemoaning his fate and expecting special consideration as a Negro. He now wanted to stand on his own merit as an artist.

In 1927, the same year that saw the publication of *Copper Sun* and *Caroling Dusk*, Harper and Brothers issued a special edition of *The Ballad of the Brown Girl*. There was no controversy about this attractive little book that has since become a collector's item.

With the coming of spring in 1928 many young people

in the arts were feverishly anticipating the announcement of the Guggenheim fellowship awards. There were seventy-five places for American artists and scientists with creative ability. The fortunate winners would spend a year abroad in study or research. The awesome committee of judges included the presidents of Radcliffe and Hamilton colleges, and professors from Harvard and the Universities of Minnesota and California.

The judges decided that Countee Cullen's verses in his three volumes of poetry were evidences of a talent worthy of encouragement. So he received one of the writing fellowships. Almost as exciting to Countee as his own appointment was the news that another Negro writer, Eric Walrond, had received a fellowship too. Eric's selection had been based on his novel, *Tropic Death*, his short stories and articles, and a romantic history of the Panama Canal. The latter work, *The Big Ditch*, had an added touch of authenticity because Walrond had lived and attended public school in the Canal Zone.

Another 1928 Guggenheim fellow was the dramatist Paul Green. In 1927, his play, *In Abraham's Bosom*, had won the Pulitzer Prize. This drama became a popular vehicle for Negro actors, and so Paul Green, a white North Carolinian, earned a place of respect among Harlemites.

But Countee Cullen was in for even more excitement than the fellowship announcements provided. About three o'clock in the afternoon on Monday, April 9, 1928, a crowd began to gather on Seventh Avenue near Salem Methodist Episcopal Church. The daughter of Dr. DuBois and the son of Dr. Cullen were to be married at six o'clock. The early arrivals found vantage points on the sidewalk, on neighbors' steps, and on the grassy strip that divided the broad avenue. By six o'clock more than a thousand people had congregated in the area. Some stormed the church entrances hoping to get the few seats not reserved for the thirteen hundred invited guests. While these outsiders waited, rumors spread through the crowd.

Someone had heard there would be sixteen bridesmaids. There were various estimates of the cost of the wedding and reception. Live canaries in gilded cages were supposed to sing throughout the ceremony. The ushers were all poets. Many famous white guests were expected. (At this there was much jostling and standing on tiptoe to get a glimpse of the celebrities.) The groom's father and another minister from Brooklyn would officiate. It was hard to separate truth from rumor.

For Yolande and Countee the thirty-six hours before the ceremony were filled with excitement. A special car had brought the sixteen bridesmaids from Baltimore. Eleven of them were members of the Moles, a social club to which Yolande belonged. The other five were her particular friends. All were graduates of Eastern colleges. Several were daughters of men who were known as Negro leaders. For example, there was Harriet Pickens, whose father had been dean of Morgan College and later became field secretary of the NAACP. And Constance Murphy came from a family of journalists who controlled the Baltimore *Afro-American*.

As they assembled at the church on Friday for the wedding rehearsal, even these sophisticated young ladies were impressed by the male attendants. They recognized the handsome best man, Harold Jackman. He was the light-skinned London-born teacher who was already gaining a reputation for his interest in the Negro theater and his collection of books, playbills, and manuscripts. And among the ten ushers they saw writer Langston Hughes making jokes about his rented formal clothes, and the modest author and teacher, Arna Bontemps. Robert C. Weaver, another usher, was still a student at Harvard, but already he had begun to earn the reputation for scholarship in the field of economics that would lead to his later positions as Rent Administrator for the State of New York and Federal Housing Administrator.

When the chattering of the young people had subsided enough for the rehearsal to begin, Dr. DuBois himself directed the proceedings. He stressed that this was no ordinary wedding. He saw it as a pageant symbolic of the beauty and power of a new breed of American Negro.

On the night before the wedding Countee held his bachelor dinner, fittingly enough, in The Dark Tower. The girls, too, had a night of sleepless merriment. But on the big day all looked as fresh and happy as they should. Dr. DuBois's plan was executed with perfection. As the gifted organist Dr. Melville Charleton played the stately wedding music and the birds trilled their accompaniment, the procession moved down the aisle. While three thousand people watched intently, Countee and Yolande exchanged their marriage vows. Among the guests were Alain Locke, James Weldon Johnson, Eugene Kinckle

Jones, Charles S. Johnson, and Miss Mary White Ovington, a benefactor of the NAACP.

The newlyweds left for a brief wedding trip to Philadelphia, Atlantic City, and Great Barrington, Massachusetts. Then Yolande returned to her teaching position in the Douglass High School in Baltimore, and Countee went back to his desk at *Opportunity*.

CHAPTER
IX

CRIES OF "Vivie la France" and strains of "The Marseillaise" rang across the Place de la Concorde in Paris. Countee nervously adjusted his new beret as he worked his way around the edge of the surging crowd. Near the Obelisk a small group of musicians began to play "The Peanut Vendor." A French housewife grasped the astonished Countee by the arm and they joined the hilarious dancing. From the Arc de Triomphe came the sound of fireworks, and rockets lighted the sky. The Parisians were celebrating Bastille Day, and Countee was witnessing this event for the first time in his life.

Without hesitation, in June, 1928, he had chosen Paris as headquarters for study and writing under his Guggenheim fellowship grant. Countee had applied for the grant while he was working at *Opportunity*. When he was notified that he had been appointed a fellow, he wound up his editorial duties as soon as he could and, alone, left New York on the last day of June. In Paris he hoped to complete a group of narrative poems and perhaps to write a libretto for an opera.

On the liner *Paris* as he lolled in his steamer chair, his eye following the perfect curve of the horizon, many problems were troubling him. First was Yolande's absence. Before he won the fellowship she had agreed to work with her friend Harriet Pickens as a counselor at Fern Rock, a YWCA camp on Bear Mountain up the Hudson in New York State. But she promised to join him later in Paris.

He had cause for concern. They were spending less time together now than they had during their courtship. Countee was not unaware of some of the talk that had been going on. He knew that some of Salem's members had thought the DuBois girl was haughty. And the relationship between his father and Yolande was less warm than he had hoped it would be. Ma, of course, could get along with anyone. Like Mrs. DuBois she remained quietly in the background. But Pa was active and accustomed to having his son accompany him when he traveled. Then too, each of the young people was an only child, and Yolande in particular (from Countee's point of view) found it hard to adjust to the compromises necessary in a marriage. It seemed a little unreasonable of her to take the job at Fern Rock. On the other hand, his income as a Guggenheim fellow was hardly sufficient for him to insist on her not working.

Then there was his own commitment to the Guggenheim Foundation. Already the idea of an opera was giving way to plans for a long narrative poem symbolic of the tragedy of the black race.

And now as he found himself dancing in the streets of Paris on the fourteenth of July, Countee was aware of another symbol. To him France meant freedom from the race consciousness he had known at home. No one here seemed to notice the color of his skin. He was surprised that the seat next to him at a restaurant did not remain conspicuously vacant throughout the meal. He was neither catered to nor ignored. He was treated as just another person.

But, he reflected, America had its own wonderful moments too; for example, he recalled that memorable day in April shortly before his marriage when he received a letter from Helen Keller, the famous deaf and blind writer and lecturer. Earlier he had enjoyed the privilege of visiting this remarkable lady at her Connecticut home. Her letter came in response to his note of appreciation sent along with his poem "For Helen Keller." His closing lines were:

> Her finer alchemy converts
> The clanging brass to golden-pealed,
> And for her sight the black earth spurts
> Hues never thought there unrevealed.

Miss Keller said of the poem that its words had "magic to turn my prison-house into a Garden of Delight." She had praise also for Cullen's first book, *Color*.

Paris in the 1920's was a magnet drawing many fascinating personalities. Josephine Baker, then a little known entertainer, had migrated there from St. Louis to become a star at the Folies Bergeres. The French capital also attracted such towering literary figures as Ernest Hemingway and F. Scott Fitzgerald, Ezra Pound, James Joyce and James Thurber. And it was at Le Bourget Field on the outskirts of Paris that Charles Lindbergh had set down his *Spirit of St. Louis* on the night of May 21, 1927, to complete his pioneer nonstop flight across the Atlantic.

In this atmosphere many young painters, sculptors, and writers believed they could contribute to the growing resurgence of interest in Negro culture. Sooner or later they would meet in the offices of the American Express on the rue Scribe, or in someone's studio, or in a café. Countee enjoyed trading progress reports with Palmer Hayden, painting one of his many seascapes, or Augusta Savage, vigorously molding or chiseling a statue, or Eric Walrond, militantly creating a novel.

Cullen's own living quarters consisted at first of a room in the Trianon on the Avenue du Maine. In this little family hotel the proprietor was also the concierge, and his son was general handyman. A neat little sign at the registration desk said "English Spoken," but Countee already knew better than to rely heavily on this promise. The proprietor's son was the supposed linguist, and he made up in smiles and gestures for what he lacked in English vocabulary.

The cleanliness of the place compensated for the absence of luxury. Countee soon became accustomed to having his bath prepared in the large bathroom down the hall. Since the hotel charged seven francs for each bath, the management made sure that the guest received his money's worth. So Countee found the huge old-fashioned tub filled nearly to the brim with piping hot water, leaving precious little space for the bather.

A continental breakfast served in his room cost less than a bath, only five francs. Countee looked forward each morning to the rich warm croissants and the coffee served with hot milk.

Outside, the street invited exploration. Countee discovered that a brisk walk south and east led him to the beautiful Montsouris Park. If he went in the opposite direction past the Montparnasse Cemetery, he could cross over to the Boulevard Raspail and go on to the Luxembourg Palace (converted into a museum) surrounded by its famed gardens. Here he joined the spectators watching small boys and their fathers sailing toy boats on the clear little lake. Nearby, right off the Boulevard Saint-Michel, was the Sorbonne where Countee planned to study French literature.

He had fun finding his way around the city. He learned to take a number and "queue up" on the line awaiting the bus. He was surprised to find that city transportation was available in first, second, and third classes. For six francs you could buy a little booklet of tickets good for rides on the Metro, tram, or omnibus. The Metro was the quickest way to get away from Montparnasse, the Latin Quarter, and the Left Bank. This underground railway had clean, spacious white-tiled stations and fast comfortable trains. It was a decided contrast to the New York subway.

Over on the Right Bank of the Seine the broad, tree-lined Champs Elysées led from the Louvre to the Arc de

Triomphe. And farther north lay the Montmartre section dominated by the famed dome of Sacré-Coeur.

Getting acquainted with Paris led to some amusing experiences. One of these involved the Bal Blomet. Some Harlem friends had earlier discovered this unique dance hall, and Countee was eager to go there. Their taxi, an aging Citroen, staggered into the narrow rue Blomet. Number 33 was an unpretentious structure scarcely wider than the outstretched arms of the average man. Beneath a sign that read "Bal Negre" they joined the line for tickets. Then they passed through a flimsy wooden door onto the noisy dance floor.

From the balcony provided for watchers Countee studied the gyrations of the dancers. The clientele consisted mainly of Martiniquais, Negro people from the French-owned island in the Caribbean. They were dancing the beguine, a native dance with a Latin-like rhythm. (Cole Porter's inspiration for "Begin the Beguine" is said to have come from watching the Martinique people dance.) Native gourds and drums accented the beat. Countee was fascinated. In a flash he descended the narrow stairs and, finding a willing partner, was soon dancing the beguine like a native.

The summer of 1928 was a period of adjustment to his surroundings and association with the summer visitors to Paris. One of the most important of these visitors was Dr. Cullen on his annual vacation trip to Europe. Countee went to Le Havre to meet his father. There he saw some "light ladies" soliciting on the street. In a poem titled "The

Street Called Crooked" he described this experience. He told of the women's approach and of his answer that he had a better lady waiting for him at home. But in sympathy he threw them a coin and tossed in a bit of philosophy for good measure.

Countee and his father went back to Paris and from there to Oberammergau, Germany, for the Passion Play. They also visited Berlin where they ran into Marcus Garvey and his wife. Garvey, a native of the British West Indies, had been deported from the United States to London after his unsuccessful attempt to launch a Back to Africa movement among American Negroes. He was an outspoken champion of racial equality. At first he had attracted a large following with his impassioned speeches, his uniformed organizations of "military" officers and Black Cross Nurses, and an unseaworthy boat that was to be the flagship of his Black Star Line. But his popularity faded when his finances became hopelessly tangled and he was convicted of fraud. Frederick Cullen, however, still considered Garvey his friend, for he admired the man's intellect and courage, and he sympathized with his misfortune.

The Cullens also visited London where they saw Paul Robeson in *Show Boat*. And finally after a trip to Vienna they returned to Paris and Dr. Cullen went back to the States.

Wherever they went they seemed to encounter someone they knew. Then too, Countee often met people who, having read his poetry, extended such courtesies as invitations to lunch or offers to book him for readings or to reprint his poems in their home newspapers. As a result that very summer he had poems in German translation published in *Der Abend* and *Der Tag* and in the Austrian *Arbeiter-Zeitung*.

After Dr. Cullen's departure, Yolande arrived in Paris. By this time relations between the couple had become quite strained. To make matters worse, Yolande became ill, and her father, when notified that she was in the American Hospital in Paris, made a hurried trip there in October to bring her back to New York. By November she had returned to her job in Baltimore.

Countee now had to settle down to the work for which his fellowship had been granted. At the Sorbonne he was enrolled in a course in French literature. Although he had studied French at New York University, he wanted to improve his fluency in speaking the language. So he engaged a tutor, and soon the Parisians he met were telling him that he spoke like a native.

But he knew that his studies were less important than his obligation to write. Fortunately he had friends from America who were also trying to do creative work in Paris, and this little group met often to encourage each other. The studio of Augusta Savage was a popular meeting place. This young woman, a Southerner who had studied sculpture in New York, was now in Paris on a Rosenwald grant. Her studio in the Latin Quarter was only a short walk from Countee's lodgings in the Trianon. Countee found it typical of the struggling artist's atelier described in novels and pictured in the movies.

A dreary-looking gate led from the street into a cobblestone courtyard. The studio was a large drafty room with a hazy glass skylight in the middle of the high ceiling. Augusta had decorated the room with crates and boxes draped with material and topped with her finished and unfinished pieces of sculpture. A short flight of wooden steps led to a balcony where sleeping space was provided. The sculptress had acquired a few housekeeping necessities such as a Sterno stove and some French cooking pots. With these she was always prepared to make tea for her guests if one of the fellows would run out to the courtyard to draw water from the community tap while the others pooled their precious francs and went to the corner patisserie for cakes and rolls. A table in the studio served two purposes, eating and playing belotte, a French card game. Countee was the acknowledged belotte expert, but the others never gave up hope of defeating him.

Sometimes Palmer Hayden would join the group. He was usually met with a few kidding remarks about his sea paintings, for he had done many of them, and to the uninformed viewer they seemed remarkably similar. Hayden, like Cullen, had been a Harmon award winner in 1926. His prize money was generously supplemented by an American patroness. Hale Woodruff, another painter, was also partly subsidized by a patron. He had come from Indianapolis, having worked his way through the Herron Art School there.

Augusta welcomed not only people in the fine arts but anyone she met and liked. Nightclub entertainers like Alberta Hunter, Frenchmen she met in art galleries, lonely Negro students from America, French colonials working

110

in Paris, all found their way to her modest studio. She was called upon for all kinds of advice and emergency aid. The case of the little hotel clerk from Martinique is an amusing example.

This young lady had a pretty, doll-like face surrounded by a bushy mop of crinkled hair. One day when she stopped by Miss Savage's place, Augusta was giving herself a shampoo. Her visitor watched with fascination as the sculptress produced an iron comb, heated it over a can of Sterno, and merely by combing her hair changed the kinky mass into smooth, satiny strands. The girl immediately asked if this magic could be performed on her own hair. She was having a special date that evening with her French boy friend. In fact, she was expecting him to propose. Augusta was glad to oblige, and the little clerk walked out proudly with her sleek and shining hairdo.

Later that evening the card game at Augusta's was interrupted by frantic pounding on the door. The Martinique girl stood sobbing on the threshhold. Her Frenchman, she said, had been furious about the appearance of her straightened hair and had refused to be seen with her in the street. What was she to do? She was ruined forever.

To make matters worse, Augusta was laughing so hard that the tears streamed down her face. Finally she explained to her young friend that there was nothing permanent about the Madam Walker method of hair culture. So saying she poured some water into a bowl, dunked her friend's head into it, and the unwanted coiffure was restored to its original bushiness. The next day Augusta and her friends were pleased to learn that the French gentle-

111

man and his little brown sweetheart had patched up their quarrel and become engaged.

Although Countee enjoyed going to Augusta Savage's studio, he realized that the companionship and encouragement he got there were no substitute for the hard work he had to do. Often Augusta would excuse herself and leave her guests to their own devices while she modeled her clay, oblivious of the people around her. But Countee had a refuge that afforded him the quiet he needed for his writing. It was the home of Steve and Sophie Green, a young American couple who had become interested in him through his poetry.

The Greens (his given name was really Julian) lived on the rue du Douanier near Montsouris Park. Their pink stucco house nestled like a jewel inside a stone-walled garden. Steve was said to be a nephew of the famous millionaire miser, Hetty Green, and to have inherited a part of her fortune when her estate was finally settled. He and his vivacious wife invited Countee to make their house his second home in Paris.

One of the rooms off the balcony made an ideal place for study and writing. From the window Countee could see the chestnut trees in the park and watch the slow drift of falling leaves as the autumn winds bared the branches. Whenever he wanted to write, he could come here and stay as long as he pleased. Steve and Sophie would not disturb him. So now he settled down to work in earnest on his long narrative poem, "The Black Christ."

CHAPTER

X

COUNTEE WOVE his poem from the threads of religious and racial emotions that he knew so well. "The Black Christ" is the story of a Negro boy who is lynched and who lives again after death. The unshakable religious conviction of his mother stands in contrast to the wavering faith of the boy and his brother. The younger members of the family cannot hold fast to Christianity in the face of the cruelties and prejudices around them. But the resurrection of the martyred boy causes the brother to renew his faith in Christ.

When Countee had finished his poem, he wrote beneath the title these words: "Hopefully dedicated to White America." From this poem Cullen's third volume of verse took its title. Other pieces in the book reflected the author's observations on many subjects.

One of his inspirations was the grave of the Unknown Soldier under the Arc de Triomphe. Walking toward this monument down the Champs Elysées, Countee became a part of the very life of the city. The pedestrians on the street, the variety of shops, the people sitting at sidewalk café tables, the waiters, the flower sellers, all reminded him how truly representative the Unknown Soldier was. Cullen expressed his tribute in the poem "At the Etoile," and again in an epitaph "For the Unknown Soldier."

Another poem Countee included in this volume contained his reaction to the Sacco-Vanzetti case. Countee had been only a high school student in 1920 when Nicola Sacco and Bartolomeo Vanzetti were arrested in Massachusetts for robbery and murder. Their trial had lasted seven years. Then in 1927, the two men were convicted and executed. At first the general public, Countee included, had shown little interest in this crime. Only after the trial proceeded did people begin to believe that the defendants' radical and anarchistic persuasions influenced the judge and jury more than any evidence that they had in fact committed the crimes of which they were accused. Countee expressed his disagreement with the decision in a sonnet ending in a couplet indicting the decision in particular and capital punishment in general:

> These men who do not die, but death decree,—
> These are the men I should not care to be.

The first poem in the book (following six pages of lines to three friends to whom the book was dedicated) was a tribute to Carolyn Cullen. To his mother Countee attributed the gentling influence in his life that caused him to control his wrath against his most bitter enemies and to feel sympathy for all helpless creatures.

114

The Black Christ contained forty-seven poems. It was published while Countee was still abroad, for he had received a year's extension of his Guggenheim fellowship. The book, the first of his works to be published in England, received good notices. Several reviewers compared "The Black Christ" to Masefield's "The Everlasting Mercy." Even as late as 1945, Mrs. Eleanor Roosevelt wrote in a newspaper column that she thought "The Black Christ" should be required reading for every American student as soon as he became mature enough to understand it.

Between the completion of his book and its publication Countee decided to leave Paris for a while. So on an April day in 1929, he boarded the train for Le Havre and arrived there in time to make connections with his steamer. He was headed for London. But before he reached Southampton on the other side of the English Channel, he began to doubt the wisdom of his decision. Although this was not his first crossing, the channel seemed rougher than he had remembered it. Even the dining salon did not offer him much comfort, but it was a refuge from the icy spray with which the churning waters flooded the deck.

From his compartment window on the train from Southampton to London he could see less and less of the countryside through the gathering fog. And when he arrived at the station, he buttoned his topcoat against the cold and stood shivering while he got his bearings and found the card on which he had written the address of the boarding house a friend had recommended.

The cab driver let him out in front of one of the many identical stone houses on Russell Square just behind the British Museum. His room offered little solace from the cold. Even after he had deposited a penny in the gas slot, the resulting heat was only partially effective against the bone-chilling dampness. Countee thought of the lines, "Oh to be in England now that April's there." He felt cheated. He found no lilacs in Kew, and he did not hear the song of a single bird.

But a few days after his arrival a friend invited him to spend a long weekend in the county of Surrey to the south. The distance of a few miles was enough to dispel the cold and gloom that had plagued him in London. The English countryside fulfilled his expectations. In a delightful essay written for *The Crisis* he described his experience. He told of the bright green grass, the golden crocuses, the yellow-beaked blackbird. He extolled the cry of the chiffchaff and the song of the lark as he heard them that Sunday morning on the way to a small thirteenth-century church.

Countee returned to London in a lighter mood. He found new lodgings on Edgeware Road. Now he could enjoy the daily bustle of the city. And at night a pleasant walk past the Marble Arch brought him to Hyde Park where traditionally anyone who cared to could speak on the subject nearest his heart. The orators usually chose either politics or religion. Countee found these harangues lively and entertaining. What is more, the evenings spent in Hyde Park were no drain on his budget.

Then Countee began to meet English people who

charmed him. Among these new acquaintances he counted Quakers John Fletcher and Winifred Cramp, novelist Winifred Holtby, poet Humbert Wolfe, and writer John Galsworthy. The friends he made in London were helpful in arranging poetry readings for him. He appeared in Sydenham, a nearby London suburb, and then he went west to Bristol. And finally he had the thrilling experience of reading in the famed old university town of Oxford. Fees from these engagements were a welcome supplement to his $2500 fellowship.

But one day in a reception room at Friends House he met the most memorable person of all. She was a diminutive white-haired lady whose quiet, angelic manner gave no hint of any association with rugged adventure. To Countee's complete surprise John Fletcher introduced her as Ethelreda Lewis, author of *Trader Horn*. In 1927, when her biography of that amazing old gentleman was published, the book became so popular that it went through twelve printings in a single year. Speculation as to whether Alfred Aloysius Horn was a real person or merely a creation of the author's imagination seemed to amuse Mrs. Lewis. But Countee soon found that the greatest concern of Ethelreda Lewis was the welfare of Negroes in South Africa where she lived. She had come to London to raise money for a recreation fund on behalf of these unfortunate people. Countee expressed the hope that Mrs. Lewis, who was contemplating a trip to America, might find a heartening financial response from American Negroes.

While Countee was busy with his English lecture tour

117

in the spring of 1929, Yolande returned to Europe. She was staying in Paris at the Trianon. They exchanged letters across the Channel discussing the possibility of a reconciliation. But it soon became apparent that the marriage would end in divorce, and Yolande went back to the States.

When Countee resumed his studies in Paris in the fall of 1929, he was not in the best of spirits. In spite of his friends and his successful readings, his life was not going smoothly. He had to smile, though, as he read a clipping his father sent him in November. In an interview for the *Bronx Journal*, Dr. Cullen described a new roller-skating club he had set up for Harlem youngsters. Pa was still fighting delinquency. But Countee was touched by the reporter's description of the glow of pride in the old man's eyes at the mention of his son. Once again, it seemed, Pa had regaled a reporter with tales of his son's success as a poet, going back to high school days and adding all the details of his college training and subsequent activities. Although a father's pride was understandable, Countee sometimes wondered about the influence of men like Cullen and DuBois on their children's married life.

In addition to the troubles of Countee's private life, or because of them, his writing was not progressing to his satisfaction. He seemed to see that first bright light of his early promise fading away. He was writing now more from force of habit than from inspiration. He was plagued by the fear that he might keep on writing when he no longer had anything significant to say. He expressed this

thought in "A Wish," a poem of six lines voicing the hope
that he might have the strength to keep silent:

> My tongue not rolling futile sounds
> After my heart has had its say.

Then in February, 1930, an event took place that gave
him a much needed jolt. He was invited to visit the Irish-
American poet Padraic Colum, who was in Paris at the
time. To their rooms in the rue Eugene Marnel, Padraic
Colum and his wife had invited several Irish poets. Colum
had asked Countee to read his poetry; but the highlight
of the evening was the invigorating conversation.

Countee listened with a lively interest as they talked of
the Irish Literary Revival and of the responsibilities of
Irish authors. He agreed with those who believed that
poetry is essentially a fine art and that it should not be
used merely as propaganda. He knew that in Colum's
poetry dealing with the Irish peasant there had been no
compromise. He also found here a basis of comparison between the Irish writer's relationship to British letters and
the Negro writer's place in American literature. Countee
found no apathy among these Irishmen. Their enthusiasm
aroused in him a feeling of compunction. He himself had
produced a shamefully small amount of poetry in the past
year.

He went back to his room fired with determination. As
if in self-punishment for his unfaithfulness to the muse of
poetry he set himself the difficult task of writing in Alexandrine verse. In this rare pattern he chided himself for
his indolence and silence. Then he told how the zeal of

the Irish poets had stimulated his resolution to do better. He called his poem, "After a Visit (at Padraic Colum's where there were Irish Poets)."

As soon as the poem was finished, Countee sent a copy to Padraic Colum. The warmth of that gentleman's response was like a tonic. Countee was especially gratified to note the poet's comment on his choice of verse form: "You succeed so well in keeping up the difficult music of the Alexandrine—a measure which I think is the very metre of regret."

About a month after Cullen's evening with the Irish poets, his divorce case came up in a Paris court. On March 27, the divorce decree was granted to Yolande through her attorney. Two other American women received decrees at the same time. But when the cabled information was reported in the American press, the headlines featured the Cullens.

For a while now, Countee had seen very little of his artist friends on the Left Bank. As a columnist for the Paris edition of the *Chicago Daily Tribune* put it, "Cullen is seldom seen on the Happy Highway." The newsman, who had interviewed Countee just after the publication of *The Black Christ,* was impressed with the poet's quiet modesty and lack of idiosyncrasies.

But after his visit to Padraic Colum, Countee began to allow himself more recreation. He was now sharing a studio with Eric Walrond, a fellow Guggenheimer. Eric, encouraged by the success of his book, *Tropic Death,* was working on his second novel. His militant outgoing personality was a helpful contrast to Cullen's introspection.

Paris afforded many diversions, and for Countee music was one of the city's most enjoyable offerings. So he was pleasantly excited to learn that Paul Robeson was to sing with the Paris Symphony at the beautiful modernistic Salle Pleyel. The principal artist, a pianist-composer, was well received, and Countee appreciated his competence. But he found himself tingling with anticipation as the moment for Robeson's appearance drew near. Then suddenly there he stood, a dark giant of a man, his deep baritone voice reverberating like the pipes of an organ.

Countee knew the story of this artist's career dating from his fame as a Phi Beta Kappa student and All-American football star at Rutgers University. Robeson had gone on to study law and pass the New York bar examinations. But, convinced by his wife and friends that he had acting talent, he had joined the Provincetown Players and had achieved success both at home and abroad in several of Eugene O'Neill's plays and in Shakespeare's *Othello*. Then by chance the amazing depth and quality of his singing voice had been discovered. And now in this French concert hall Countee felt both pride and nostalgia as Paul Robeson sang Negro spirituals and German lieder. The rest of the audience was affected, too. They stood and yelled for encores and were disappointed to learn that the orchestra had no more of Robeson's music. So they shouted for him to sing alone, but in deference to the fine musicians of the orchestra he declined to sing without their accompaniment and ended the performance with a brief speech of thanks.

121

Countee's emotional ties to Harlem resulted in his be-coming an unofficial host to Negro artists and students who came to Paris. He had been there nearly two years now, and in this time he had met people in many walks of life. Professors and students at the Sorbonne, both French and foreign, had been friendly, and he enjoyed scholarly discussions with them. White American friends of Steve and Sophie Green had been pleasant, too. And his associa-tion with American, French, and English writers and ar-tists had been helpful and stimulating. But perhaps his most intimate social relationships were those with his American Negro friends and their closest white associates.

He liked to share his knowledge of the interesting places in Paris that the newcomer might not find on his own. For example, he had discovered the Lapin Agile, a café on the Left Bank in the oldest part of Paris, where in the fifteenth century Francois Villon is said to have en-joyed many a bottle of vintage wine as he recited his bal-lads. Countee also liked the *cafés chantants* where the customers provided their own entertainment by singing together the old songs that every Frenchman had known since childhood. Countee had learned some of these songs in school, and although he insisted that he had no singing voice, he readily joined in the lusty singing of "Cadet Rouselle" or "Mariane S'en Allait au Moulin."

Several cafés around Paris displayed the work of strug-gling artists. Countee delighted in finding these places and urging his friends Palmer Hayden and Hale Woodruff to take advantage of the free publicity by offering their work to the proprietors. And he dutifully patronized the nightclubs in the Montmartre section whenever artists from Harlem were appearing on the bill to add their popular jazz entertainment to the apache dancing usually featured in these places.

Other Negro visitors from the States received his kind attention, too. For example, there was a socialite from Cleveland who had commissioned Augusta Savage to make a bust of her daughter. She had met Countee at the studio and was later impressed by his efforts to enhance her visit to Paris. So, knowing his fondness for playing cards, she gave a card party at her hotel for Countee and Augusta and some of their friends.

Another example of his interest in his compatriots is a young student from Harlem. She was preparing to be a teacher of French and had come with a group from Columbia University for a semester's study at the Sorbonne. Mutual friends had suggested her getting in touch with Augusta Savage and Countee. Since her name was Augusta Emanuel they called her Little Augusta, and she became their protégée. She lived with a French family consisting of a medical student named Lucette Maire and her widowed mother.

One day, after the end of the school term, Countee, Eric, Big Augusta, several Sorbonne students, and assorted visitors had gathered at the Gare de Lyons to bid good-by to Little Augusta who was returning to New York. The young people had made a special effort to get to the station at the early morning hour. Some had even stayed up all night, fortifying themselves with coffee and onion soup. As they chatted and joked with each other the mo-

123

ments slipped by, and suddenly Countee realized that the traveler had not arrived. The station master paged the missing girl, her friends implored officials to order a delay, but the boat train left for Le Havre without her.

The breathless Augusta had a plausible explanation for her tardiness. Her friend Lucette, driving her to the station, had unfortunately chosen a route through Les Halles. Now no motorist could possibly get through the honking trucks and pyramids of meats, vegetables, fruits, and flowers that cluttered the streets when this vast market came to life in the Paris dawn. So the girls had to sit helplessly in Lucette's little Citroen and watch the hands of the big clock on the square move past departure time.

Countee, touched by his friend's anxiety, immediately took charge. At American Express they learned that passage was available on a ship leaving that day from the port of Boulogne. Countee canceled his plans for the day and busied himself with the complexities of exchanging the steamship ticket and getting Little Augusta and himself on the next train to Boulogne. In the modest third-class compartment Countee was his most entertaining self, and he soon had his companion laughing at the comic aspects of her misfortune. In Boulogne they had dinner in a small restaurant. Then, recklessly disregarding the consequences to his budget, Countee hired an open carriage and they rode in storybook style through the quaint little town until time for the ship's departure.

Not many weeks after this episode Countee realized that he himself would soon be leaving Paris. In these two years he had completed his book and had made plans for writing a play and a novel. In the course of a little more than two years he had been both married and divorced. Through it all he had experienced the heights of joy and the depths of sorrow.

CHAPTER

XI

In the fall of 1930, when Countee returned from his two years' residence abroad, he found that some changes were taking place in New York. The stock market panic of 1929 had been reported in Europe, of course, but the Negro artists and writers in Paris had not been greatly alarmed. After all, they could not lose what they had never owned. But now in New York Countee saw that the Great Depression had begun. People were complaining about the scarcity of jobs. Some of his friends in the professions of law and medicine noted that business was very slow because people just did not have the money to pay for their services. Friends in the literary arts began to wonder how their chances for publication would be affected.

Talk of the depression began to permeate meetings and social events in Harlem. Countee even noticed it creeping into the general conversation before and after a program given in his honor by a club known as the Book Studio

Group. Early in September, shortly after his arrival in New York, he had been invited to this affair. It was a testimonial to his work as a poet. A feature of the evening was the gift of a scrapbook of clippings and programs concerning Cullen and his poetry. Arthur Schomburg, avid book collector, writer, and historian, had compiled the scrapbook and made the presentation. Countee was touched by the large number of friends and acquaintances, both Negro and white, who had come to welcome him home. He recognized Heywood Broun, the famous journalist. Walter White was there, too. The very presence of this NAACP leader recalled to Countee's mind the stories he had heard in his boyhood of Mr. White's exciting adventures in the South observing and investigating lynchings, unrecognized as a Negro because of his white skin and Nordic features. White was also the author of a successful novel, *The Fire in the Flint*. The writing profession was further represented by George S. Schuyler, the controversial Negro journalist, and by Wallace Thurman, a brilliant novelist. Thurman had been known to ridicule his fellow members of the Negro literati by coining the term "Niggerati" to describe them.

From the musical arts came Hall Johnson, director of a choral group famed for electrifying interpretations of the spirituals; Jules Bledsoe, a baritone who had been featured in *Show Boat;* and Melville Charlton, the highly trained organist who had played at Countee's wedding. Shelton Hale Bishop, Harlem's popular Episcopalian priest, was there, as was Richard Bruce Nugent, a young artist. And adding greatly to Countee's pleasure was the presence of his very good friends Rudolph Fisher, Arna Bontemps, and Harold Jackman.

This occasion bolstered Cullen's determination to persevere in his work. He turned his thoughts to writing a novel. In it he planned to show the two faces of Harlem. He would juxtapose plebeian characters and members of sophisticated Harlem society. He would feature the Negro church as a backdrop to the dramatic events of his story.

Countee usually worked best when he had an occasional diversion. He often enjoyed the company of friends who were not writers. One such person was Harry Roberson, a postal employee who, like other government workers, was free from the depression jitters. Harry sometimes attended A'Leilia Walker Robinson's parties, and it was there one night that he casually introduced Countee to his sister, Ida Mae. She had come from Kansas City with her older sister to visit their brothers. The Robersons, a large family, were Oklahomans who had moved to Kansas City where the children had been reared and educated. Harry and his brother Orlando, a professional singer, had migrated to New York. Countee noticed that Ida was quiet almost to shyness, her petite figure enhanced by the soft, pleasant quality of her speaking voice. Later as he looked back on their meeting he remembered his subconscious feeling that this moment was to become more important than it seemed at the time.

One evening in early spring, as Countee put aside his novel for the day, he looked around his study in the Salem parsonage at 2190 Seventh Avenue. It was a pleasant, comfortable room, and at times he was loath to leave it.

The collection of books on shelves around the room had grown considerably since his early college days. He had placed a plump hassock in the corner for the daily naps of his favorite cat. Interesting prints and paintings adorned the walls.

But tonight he had a special engagement downtown. Meticulously groomed he hurried into the fresh spring air. He enjoyed the brisk walk to the subway but was annoyed to find how stale the air was when he descended to the subway platform. At the same time he was looking forward to the literary reception to which he had been invited. He wondered who would be there.

Arriving at his destination Countee smiled and exchanged greetings as he worked his way through the gathering of writers, publishers, and members of the press. He had spied his friend Arna Bontemps, who was one of the honored guests at this reception for authors of first novels. He offered enthusiastic congratulations, and they were soon deep in a discussion of his friend's success. Countee had read the reviews of *God Sends Sunday* in the *Herald Tribune,* the *Times,* and the *Saturday Review of Literature.* But Bontemps was most excited about the comments of Laurence Stallings, then book columnist for the *New York Sun.*

For a number of years Stallings had been highly regarded in literary circles. Theater-goers knew him as coauthor with Maxwell Anderson of the popular war drama *What Price Glory.* Then his scenario for the war film, *The Big Parade,* had spread his fame among movie lovers. He was well prepared to write bitterly and realistically about war, for he had lost a leg as a result of battle wounds received in France in 1918.

In spite of his success as a playwright, Stallings did not forsake his career as a journalist. He was a critic whose judgments were highly respected. Was it any wonder, then, that Arna Bontemps was elated by his favorable review?

As Cullen and Bontemps talked, the latter confided that he was curious to meet Mr. Stallings. Just then their conversation was interrupted by Captain Stallings himself. He was a relaxed and friendly man distinguished by a wealth of graying hair. Countee, who already knew the famous critic, introduced Bontemps.

Naturally they discussed *God Sends Sunday*. Stallings suggested that Bontemps should get someone to dramatize the novel. As he went on to give his reasons, his listeners visualized the dramatic impact the novel's hero, Little Augie, might have on a theater audience.

For days after the reception Countee could not get *God Sends Sunday* out of his mind. Finally he went over to Arna Bontemp's house and suggested that they collaborate on rewriting the book as a play. Both men agreed to start at once. They had to work fast because Bontemps was leaving for the West Coast in August, and Countee was going abroad again. His father's annual vacation time was approaching and, as usual, Countee was to be his traveling companion and interpreter. Before the summer was over Bontemps and Cullen had finished their revision, and the play began a long and uncertain career.

The young authors were realistic enough to know that

in this period of depression they had little chance for a Broadway production of their drama. So they were content to see it launched in Cleveland at Karamu House, a new community center devoted to the arts. Then they secured Leah Salisbury as an agent. This was indeed a stroke of fortune, for Miss Salisbury handled some of the best known names in the writing profession.

A few years later the Federal Theater was formed to provide work for unemployed actors. The New York division of this project, headed by Orson Welles and other theatrical powers, took an option on the play. From this source Bontemps and Cullen received small checks at regular intervals until the New York wing of the Federal Theater was abolished.

Meanwhile the Los Angeles branch of the Federal Theater became interested. However, the leaders there felt that the play should be expanded to include additional characters, thus providing work for more actors. They engaged Langston Hughes to make the necessary changes, but no sooner had the production date been set than the Federal Theater was abolished in Los Angeles. The ill-fated play met the same fortune in Chicago.

Finally, Miss Salisbury interested Edward Gross in producing God Sends Sunday. But Mr. Gross was convinced that it should be presented as a musical. So Bontemps and Cullen did it over, both going out to California to work with Harold Arlen and Johnny Mercer, the famous songwriting team. In its musical form the story was known as St. Louis Woman. After a tryout of five weeks on the road, the production finally reached the Martin Beck Theater on Broadway in April, 1946.

In New York, *St. Louis Woman* ran 113 performances. It introduced Pearl Bailey and also included the Nicholas Brothers and Rex Ingram in its cast. An adaptation called *Free and Easy* was done in Amsterdam, Paris, and Brussels. The movie rights were sold to MGM, but the picture was never produced.

In the summer of 1931, as soon as Countee had completed his part in the dramatization of *God Sends Sunday,* he left for Paris. He went ahead of his father, and by the sixth of July he was enrolled in a summer course at the Sorbonne.

He was puzzled at first to see the streets of Paris filled with dark-complexioned strangers. Then he discovered that many of these people were there in connection with the Colonial Exposition. The Asian and African colonies of several countries were represented by buildings in the huge area set aside for this purpose. Among the most spectacular were a replica of Indo-China's Temple of Angkor and the Belgian Congo pavilion. There were also dazzling gold exhibits from Dahomey and intricate carvings from the Ivory Coast. But the most interesting products from these faraway lands were the people—delicately beautiful girls from Indo-China, handsome black giants from Senegal, and Moroccans in their fezzes—all adding color and gaiety to the city.

In spite of the holiday atmosphere Countee had to concentrate on his studies. He had found living quarters on the rue de l'Ecole de Medecine, near the ancient Sorbonne. The buildings that he passed on his daily walks to school were conducive to a serious attitude. The dingy lycées where secondary school students prepared for their stiff college entrance exams were stern reminders of the importance of mental discipline. Nor was there anything frivolous about the classic architecture of the Pantheon with its carved inscription above the entrance proclaiming it to be a monument from a grateful country to its great men.

Countee supplemented his literature courses at the university with a continuation of his private lessons in French conversation. He was also working on his novel. But he always reserved some time for fun. As usual a number of American Negroes were summering in Europe, and Countee spent many pleasant hours with them. On a typical night they could be found in a café playing belotte, eating and drinking and talking. Most of these friends were interested in the arts. Harold Jackman was there on his vacation from teaching. The painters Hale Woodruff and Palmer Hayden had luckily found the means to remain in Paris. Two girls from Boston enlivened the group. They were "Toki" Schalk, a columnist for the Negro newspaper *The Pittsburgh Courier,* and her friend, Doris Dandridge. Other friends were Bill White, son of Clarence Cameron White, the noted violinist, and Harold Dingwall, glowing from his recent engagement to a French girl.

The presence of so many visitors to Paris prompted Steve and Sophie Green to suggest a party at their home in late July. Countee busied himself writing notes to all the summer tourists he knew. They were to arrive "on Friday night—any time after ten and before three." These hours were selected, he said, so that "you can come even if you have another engagement." And everybody came, including the Greens' personal friends.

The house was a perfect setting for a party. The spacious two-storied living room was filled with a large assortment of people. At a table on the balcony an Austrian count played cards with a prince from Dahomey. At other tables, Americans from Chicago, Indiana, West Virginia, and Harlem exchanged travel experiences while they feasted on strange delicacies prepared by a Japanese cook. Waiters passed through the crowd offering champagne. Some of the guests amused themselves by looking over the balustrade at the people who had congregated on the polished floor that had been cleared for dancing to the music of a Negro jazz orchestra.

There were teachers, artists, attorneys, writers, musicians, and socialites. Their hosts, Steve, Sophie, and Countee, were all over the place making sure that not a single guests went unnoticed. And no one had a better time than Countee.

During the week following the party Countee studied with renewed energy. It was now early August and he had to prepare for his examinations and make plans for his father's arrival. He often regretted that Mrs. Cullen had never overcome her fear of travel, for he knew there were many attractions here, especially the fine music, that she would have enjoyed. But it seemed that he was destined to take charge of Pa's vacations. And he realized that he was fortunate, indeed, to be able to spend so much time in France, a country he was growing to regard with great affection. Thanks to the church, the Guggenheim Foundation, his parents' contributions, and his own frugal savings from royalties, lectures fees, and odd jobs, he had spent three consecutive summers here.

This year's vacation had been very rewarding. The change of scene had enabled him to take stock of himself, to study, to write, and to play. And later he was gratified to note that, despite his socializing, his postexamination certificate from the Sorbonne was marked with a special commendation for excellence.

CHAPTER

XII

Eıgнт нundred poetry lovers listened intently on a Monday night in 1931 as Countee Cullen read. In Sayles Hall on the campus of Brown University in Providence, Rhode Island, the warmth and intensity of his voice made his hearers forget the December cold outside. He was the second in a series of Marshall Woods lecturers. Cullen began by reading a passionate plea for Negro dignity in the face of humiliation and suffering. This was Claude McKay's "If We Must Die." Then he read "The Creation," James Weldon Johnson's beautiful version of the *Genesis* story written as a poetic Negro sermon. From the verses of Langston Hughes, Cullen had chosen two poems. The first, "The Negro Speaks of Rivers," links the black race historically with some of the world's great rivers—the Euphrates, the Congo, the Nile, and the Mississippi. In contrast he read Hughes' "Mother to Son," in which a mother urges her son to persevere against the hardships he must endure as a Negro.

Finally the speaker came to his own poems. His audience drew closer in spirit as they watched the youthful brown face of the man who stood before them. Many of these people had never known a young intellectual Negro. Now they felt that here was a personal friend ready to share all the beauty, the learning, the love, the hurt, the laughter that had touched his life in twenty-eight years.

He began with "Heritage," the lines ringing with the rich imagery of an African background. In these verses the audience could sense the emotional conflict of pagan and Christian influences. The opening question, "What is Africa to me?" sounded the alert. Careful listeners heard the poet enumerate the passions that he owed to a 300-year-old pagan culture. He mentioned the song of the "wild barbaric birds," the throbbing rhythm of African drums, and his emotional response to the sound of rain. Later in the poem he spoke of his difficulty in curbing a pagan impulse to express anger and impatience with the woes he suffered as a black man in a Christian civilization. In the closing lines of the poem he said:

> Not yet has my heart or head
> In the least way realized
> They and I are civilized.

Then, abandoning the racial theme, Cullen explained his next poem. He told of his long-standing admiration for the poetry of John Keats and gave a little of the English poet's biography. Then he read "To John Keats, Poet at Spring Time," and the lines seemed to confirm the fact that he was a kindred spirit of his ideal poet. He ended the session on a lighter note with several of his witty epitaphs. There were four-line poems that he liked to write, sometimes in praise, but often in satire. In one of them he pictures Amy Lowell boldly confronting God across a golden table:

> She leans across a golden table,
>   Confronts God with an eye
> Still puzzled by the standard label
>   All flesh bears: Made to die—
> And questions Him if He is able
>   To reassure her why.

Another tells of a mouthy woman:

> God and the devil still are wrangling
>   Which should have her, which repel;
> God wants no discord in his heaven;
>   Satan has enough in hell.

It had been a rewarding experience, as his reading engagements usually were. Yet the cordial response of his audiences never ceased to amaze him. And on the way home he thought again of his often stated paradox that these lyrical outpourings should come from a poet whom God had seen fit to make black.

The year 1932 began with a pleasant outlook for Countee. In February, his novel, *One Way to Heaven*, was published. The reviews were encouraging. In the *Herald Tribune's Books* his friend Rudolph Fisher wrote that Cullen had successfully met the challenge of a poet turned novelist. Other reviewers made favorable mention of the pathos and readability of the book.

In spite of a life that he himself had once called secluded and uneventful, Countee was well acquainted with Harlem, the scene of his story. Not only was he accustomed to the Negro society represented in his novel by the wealthy Constancia Brandon, but he also knew humble people like her dark-skinned housemaid, Mattie Johnson. He knew, too, the kind of revival meeting where Mattie met the rascally Sam Lucas. To Countee the oft-repeated story of his father's conversion was now as familiar as if he had been there himself. And he realized that for every pretender like Sam, there were hundreds of true believers like the fictitious Mattie Johnson and the real Frederick Cullen who came to the altar at the evangelist's invitation.

The action of *One Way to Heaven* begins on a "watch meeting" night. This is the night of December 31, when the churches open their doors to those who wish to watch the old year out and the new year in. It is a profitable time for revivalists. On this night the churches are usually filled with sinners and backsliders whose churchgoing is ordinarily confined to Easter, Mother's Day, and New Year's Eve. On many such occasions Countee had joined in the familiar hymns, listened to the trite but sincere testimonies of the practicing Christians, and watched the expressions on the faces of the new converts. So he was able to make these scenes in his story strikingly realistic.

In his novel he could not resist poking a little fun at the "arty" soirees held in the Brandons' home on "Striver's

Row," the Harlemites' familiar name for the street where the more prosperous residents lived. In an earlier novel, *Nigger Heaven* (1926), Countee's friend Carl Van Vechten had depicted Harlem life in a similar way. Unfortunately many Negroes, offended by the title, had never read Van Vechten's book, thus missing the author's sympathetic treatment of his theme. Some critics of *One Way to Heaven* thought that Cullen had been influenced by Van Vechten.

But in general, Countee's novel went well. And even people who were not primarily interested in literature read the book to try to identify the characters as people they knew. Of course, they could not prove their suspicions since the frontispiece bore the disclaimer: "Some of the characters in this book are fictitious."

Many Negro writers of this period were now authoring novels. Most of these books had Negro themes with settings either in Harlem or in the South. Claude McKay had written *Home to Harlem* in 1928, Langston Hughes' *Not Without Laughter* came out in 1930, George Schuyler, a journalist, wrote the fantastic *Black No More* in 1931, and in the same year Bontemps' *God Sends Sunday* appeared. But the work of Wallace Thurman was perhaps the furthest removed from that of Cullen. While Countee's *One Way to Heaven* mildly satirized the Harlem elite, Thurman's novel, *Infants of the Spring*, published in the same year, was violently critical of this intellectual group. The talented Thurman was the greatest dissenter in the Renaissance movement.

*   *   *

The year that had started so auspiciously was marred by the death of Carolyn Belle Cullen on October 5, 1932. After an illness of only four days she left as quietly as she had lived. Now a sober stillness fell on the parsonage, enveloping the husband and son who remained there.

The preceding summer had found the Cullen men as usual in Europe. Countee left early enough to enroll at the Sorbonne. He had begun to consider a teaching career. In fact, the principal of a New York junior high school had written him an encouraging letter. Weighing his assets Countee decided that preparation in French language and literature, added to his strong background in English, should qualify him to teach in these two subject areas.

Customarily Dr. Cullen arrived in Europe for his annual vacation in July or August, and his son usually reserved that time to spend with him. But this July Countee was unable to leave his Sorbonne classes. So his friend Harold Jackman accompanied the older man to Athens, a city Dr. Cullen had long wanted to visit.

In his study of French literature Countee became acquainted with the poetry of Charles Pierre Baudelaire. The unhappy life of this nineteenth-century mystic fascinated Cullen to such an extent that he was inspired to write free translations of several Baudelaire poems. In one of them the Frenchman had said that death is the only real consolation a mortal may expect as he travels through this sorrowful world. Countee carefully shaped this disturbing thought into an English sonnet. He called it "Death to the Poor."

But he had a closer link with Baudelaire: an interest in

cats. On this subject Countee fashioned two sonnets translating the French poet's portrayal of the cat as a noble, independent, mysterious creature.

While he worked on these translations and on a number of original sonnets, Countee was also planning his next book of poetry. Then the idea of translating began to increase its hold on him; he decided to write a new version of Euripides' *Medea*.

Cullen's decision to invade the field of drama was influenced by several factors. Among them were his successful collaboration with Arna Bontemps and his compelling interest in the theater. Then too, one of his favorite players was Rose McClendon, a veteran Negro actress who most recently had starred on Broadway in Paul Green's play, *In Abraham's Bosom*. Countee believed that Mrs. McClendon had the talent and temperament for the role of the Greek heroine. He could visualize her portrayal of the beauty, horror, coquetry, and pathos associated with this character. So he wrote his version of the play with her in mind, hoping to show that the universality of human emotions transcends race.

Right along with these serious thoughts and plans Countee was able to include the worldly pleasures that made him seem like a paradox to some of his acquaintances. For example, in August, 1932, he wrote to a friend that Paris was still the world's paradise and that he was enjoying every minute of the day and night. He had danced the beguine, played belotte, and loved a little. He could ask for nothing more.

* * *

By March, 1933, when President Franklin D. Roosevelt took office, the depression had resulted in a breakdown of the nation's banking system and the President had promptly closed all the banks. Harlemites who had predicted that things would get worse before they got better saw this as the last straw. They now looked to the New Deal for economic opportunities. They believed that their chances for employment would be better with the new federal agencies than with private employers. They welcomed the heartening news that projects for writers, actors, and laborers were soon to be established. And indeed many Negroes were employed in the Federal Writers' Project.

Countee, however, was not one of them. By now he was thoroughly convinced that he needed a permanent job to supplement his income from writing and lecturing. He was by no means ready to abandon his literary career, for he still had many ideas that he wanted to get on paper. And periodically he received interesting mail and encouraging offers. A letter of commendation from Pearl Buck had been one of his recent acquisitions. And he had also received a tentative offer to collaborate on rewriting his novel as an opera, and another to produce it as a play.

But in December of 1934, Countee Cullen began his career as a teacher. He was assigned to Frederick Douglass Junior High School 139 as a regular teacher of French. The building was much like the one in which Countee himself had studied as a boy. It was an aging structure situated on 140th Street in the heart of Harlem. In keeping with the tradition in New York City public schools, boys and girls attended separate classes and there were clearly marked entrances for each sex. A paved play yard surrounded the school on three sides, and the entire area was enclosed by a high chain-link fence.

Mr. Cullen did not look particularly like either a teacher or a poet as he reported for duty that first day. Although he was now thirty-one years old, his boyish expression made him appear younger. He never wore a hat, and his hair was the color and texture Negroes sometimes called "meriney," a crinkly reddish tan. His skin was somewhat darker. His eyes could best be described as "earnest," though a closer look revealed a mischievous twinkle in their brown depths. He was not very tall, and his figure was somewhat plump from the gourmet dishes he had learned to love in France.

Countee bounded up the steps to the main entrance and turned toward the principal's office. Soon he found himself being escorted to his classroom where the principal introduced him to his pupils. At first glance he could recognize a challenge that would tax every bit of his versatility and ingenuity. These boys from deep Harlem, ranging in age from twelve to fifteen years, did not seem likely candidates for the study of a foreign language.

He remembered the tales Pa had told of his own experiences as a teacher so long ago in the country town of Fairmount, Maryland. Now he could understand how Frederick Cullen, young, idealistic, and fresh from his studies at Morgan, had felt as he faced his first class. Pa had later confessed that he became a teacher as a second choice because he doubted his worthiness to answer the call to

144

the ministry. Countee wondered if his own choice of teaching was an admission of failure as a poet. But on the practical side he knew he had to earn a living, and he resolved to be a good and devoted teacher.

To Countee's surprise the boys at 139 were intrigued with the idea of speaking French. Of course, they wanted to acquire this facility with the least possible effort. But their teacher was determined to capture their attention, and soon the pupils were listening wide-eyed to the tales of his experiences among the French people. There were some who doubted that Mr. Cullen had actually lived in this far-off place, but even they were entranced with his new and different stories. Before long a few of the boys tried to write some verse—in French.

Teaching was a harder job than Countee had imagined it would be. He had been at 139 only a short time when some English classes were added to his schedule. So he usually spent his weekday evenings in his studio at the parsonage conscientiously grading papers and looking forward to the weekend. He soon discovered that he was not alone in his attitude. Two young women, Louise Logan and Margaret Douglass, confided that they too belonged to the "Thank goodness, it's Friday" club. Drawn together by their common experiences as novice teachers, the three became fast friends.

On Fridays after school they usually found a way to celebrate the fact that they had survived another week. Often they played bridge. Harold Jackman, now an experienced teacher, made a welcome fourth. And on one occasion they even allowed themselves the extravagance of dining at the Colony restaurant, famous for its elegance and for the celebrities who could sometimes be seen there.

But Countee had to spend much of his precious spare time preparing his latest book for publication. It was *The Medea and Some Poems.*

Medea, the classic story of a woman scorned, as told in a drama by Euripides, had been translated from the Greek by many writers. In his version, Cullen tried to make the spoken lines readable and realistic, so he wrote them in prose. But he wrote the choruses as lyrical poems, and Virgil Thompson, an accomplished composer, set them to music.

The rest of the book contained a number of poems mostly written in France. "After a Visit" was one of these, and the Baudelaire translations, "Death to the Poor" and the two "cat" sonnets were included too. Then he had written two sonnets to France. In one of them he spoke of the magic of Paris and of its power to heal his sadness. As he put it, he

> . . . found across a continent of foam
> What was denied my hungry heart at home.

In the other sonnet to France he spoke of his dream of spending the last days of his life in that beautiful country. And in France he had also composed several love sonnets that he included in the book.

The outstanding protest poem in the volume was "Scottsboro, Too, Is Worth Its Song," a poem to American poets. In it he criticized the poets for ignoring the tragedy of the nine Negro boys whose long, drawn-out trial in the

South had been so widely publicized. He ended the poem with these lines:

> Surely, I said
> Now will the poets sing.
>> But they have raised no cry.
>> I wonder why.

At the end of the school term in June, 1935, Countee felt that this year more than ever he really deserved his European vacation. He was exhausted enough to relax completely. In Paris the French artist Renan caught him in this carefree mood and produced a portrait that became Countee's favorite. Monsieur Renan, who was hard of hearing, did not annoy his subject with unnecessary conversation. So Countee sat happily in his red and white checked shirt and scarlet tie. On his head perched a green felt hat that he had carefully maneuvered into an original shape. Renan had caught the sparkle in his eye, and the entire canvas revealed Cullen's love of fun.

147

CHAPTER
XIII

THE YEAR 1935 was one that Countee was not likely to forget. To begin with it was the year his friend Bud Fisher died. Rudolph Fisher was a rare combination, a doctor of medicine and a brilliant writer. His was one of the popular voices of the Harlem Renaissance dealing realistically with stories of Negro life. People who read books knew him as the author of the novel *The Walls of Jericho* and numerous short stories, articles, and reviews. Other Harlemites knew him as a good-looking, friendly chap who could crowd more than twenty-four hours into a day.

The year 1935 was made still more memorable by the Harlem riots. On the nineteenth of March a relatively minor incident developed into a series of rumors that fanned the flames of violence and led to wanton destruction.

The casual pedestrian along 125th Street on this particular Tuesday afternoon saw the usual familiar sights. From Eighth Avenue he could look eastward past the food market, the ten-cent store, and the small hat and shoe shops on down to Seventh Avenue. The usual amount of paper and debris swirled in the gutters and fluttered on the sidewalks. Women on the way home from work darted into the stores for last-minute purchases. Probably none of them had any idea that today would be different from yesterday.

Suddenly a crowd appeared outside the ten-cent store, and those who could get near the doors pushed their way inside as people further back took their places. Then the rumors began. At first it was said that a Negro boy had stolen a knife in the store and that the proprietor had dragged him down into the basement and beaten him. By the time this story reached the outer edges of the crowd the boy had become a ten-year-old child killed by the proprietor for stealing candy.

The crowd degenerated into an ugly mob seeking vengeance against the storekeeper and all the privileged white people he symbolized. To add to the confusion a hearse now appeared near the store. Its arrival immediately touched off a rumor that the boy had in fact been killed and that his body was about to be removed.

Now groups of people began to roam through other Harlem streets. Some of them, unaware of how the trouble had started, were nonetheless glad to give vent to their wrath against both their real and their imagined oppressors. Many threw rocks through store windows. Others seized the opportunity to steal the merchandise unprotected inside. It was three o'clock in the morning before order could be restored. At least one man was killed, a number of people were wounded, and property damage ran high.

On Wednesday morning Countee was aware, as were all the thinking people of Harlem, that something must be done. Although he and his father were comfortably housed and fed, they knew that they were in a minority. Thousands of unemployed Negroes were frustrated by their unsuccessful attempts to get jobs in the Harlem stores where they traded in large numbers. This, most leaders agreed, was the major cause of the unrest that so easily became violent.

Some others believed that Harlemites were disturbed by the Scottsboro case. Indeed Countee himself had written a poem on this subject, and Langston Hughes had written a play, *Scottsboro Limited*. By now the Scottsboro boys had spent four years in an Alabama prison condemned to die for an uncommitted crime. And they were still there.

Every Negro in Harlem knew the story. Nine uneducated black boys aged thirteen to nineteen were riding a freight train in Alabama. Most of them did not know each other. Several white teen-agers were riding the same freight. A fight broke out between the two groups, and after the whites lost they went to the nearest town and reported that nine Negroes had raped two dungaree-clad white girls who were also riding one of the boxcars. The first nine Negroes the authorities could catch became the "Scottsboro boys." Within three weeks they were brought to trial and condemned to die.

Harlemites heard many stories of attempts by various

groups to free the boys, but now on the fourth anniversary of their arrest little progress was evident. Their plight was just another symbol of the hopelessness of the Negro cause.

On the Thursday following the Harlem riot, New York's Mayor LaGuardia announced the formation of a committee to investigate the causes of the outbreak and to recommend solutions for the problems involved. The list of eleven members was impressive. There were six Negroes: Hubert Delany, a city tax commissioner; A. Philip Randolph, president of the Brotherhood of Sleeping Car Porters; Charles E. Toney, judge of the Municipal Court; Mrs. Eunice Hunton Carter, social worker and lawyer; Dr. Charles Roberts, dentist; and Countee Cullen, author. The white members were Arthur Garfield Hays, lawyer; William Jay Schieffelin, trustee of Tuskegee University; Morris Ernst, lawyer; Oswald Garrison Villard, magazine publisher; and Dr. John J. Grimley, physician.

The masses in Harlem complained that these people belonged to the privileged class and did not understand their grievances. In spite of these protests the committee went on with its work, breaking up into subcommittees to investigate crime, unemployment, education, legislation, health, housing, labor, and relief. Countee was assigned to the education group under the chairmanship of Mr. Villard.

Meanwhile, the city officials were receiving many complaints and suggestions. One of the criticisms said that the mayor should have appointed a minister to the investigating committee. Mr. LaGuardia now tried to remedy

this omission by appearing before the Inter-Denomina-
tional Preachers' Meeting of Greater New York and Vicinity. The ministers met in Salem, Dr. Cullen's church. The
mayor asked them to help him improve conditions in Harlem and to try and make their parishioners understand the
problem. He also invited the pastors to elect one of their
members to represent them on the committee.

By August the investigating committee was ready with
a report. They began with a condemnation of the police,
accusing them of acting with "barbarity." They pointed
out the need for basic economic and social reforms, assert-
ing that discrimination and insecurity were the underly-
ing causes of the March 19 disorders. And they predicted
future eruptions if these conditions were not remedied.

The report was neatly filed. The subcommittee on education planned some radio programs, with Mrs. Roosevelt
agreeing to appear on the first one. The city built a new
playground in Harlem. And the community quieted down
to a temporary normalcy.

This had been the first important Harlem riot. There
had, of course, been demonstrations dating back to the
protest parade in 1918 that had been staged in sympathy
with the treatment of Southern Negroes. But Harlem itself
had, through the 1920's at least, been considered a desir-
able community. In 1925, ten years before the first riot,
James Weldon Johnson had written for Alain Locke's
The New Negro an essay titled "Harlem: The Culture
Capital." He referred to this community as "the greatest
Negro city in the world." He noted that Harlem was not
a slum. He pointed with pride to Negro property owner-

ship, the diversity of employment, the cordial feeling between the races, the absence of crime. And he ended the essay with the optimistic statement that he believed Harlem would remain a model of cultural and economic success.

It is hard to say what went wrong during the ten years that followed Mr. Johnson's cheerful predictions. Some writers have blamed the depression. Indeed, unemployment was still a pressing problem in Harlem, and many residents, from laborers to professionals, felt its pinch. Bob McCullough, for one, could testify to this. He was Countee's old friend and classmate at Clinton. He had studied law, was admitted to the New York bar in 1935, and had promptly opened a law office. But the depression years were not kind to him, and he fled to the safety of postal employment in order to support his wife.

Whatever the causes of unrest in Harlem, they were not eliminated after the 1935 disturbance. Instead they lay dormant until the summer of 1943, when trouble broke out again. This time the shooting of a Negro soldier by a civilian police officer touched off the riot. Although the victim was later proven to be in the wrong, the citizens of Harlem remained indignant because they had long been incensed over stories of civilian violence against Negro soldiers generally. So only a spark was needed to set off another wild period of fighting and looting.

In a book called *Riots and Ruins* published in 1945, the Reverend Adam Clayton Powell, Sr. (father of the congressman from Harlem), charged that the 1943 riot stemmed partly from the fact that the recommendations of the 1935 committee were never publicized or carried out. Walter White of the NAACP had expressed a similar view in an article written for the August 16, 1943, issue of *The New Republic*. Powell and other leaders insisted that the rioters were protesting not just the wrongs of the moment but all the combined injustices suffered by Negroes since the seventeenth century when they were brought to America as slaves.

There has been little agreement in placing the blame for these disturbances. Writers have censured the police, municipal authorities, a small percentage of delinquents, and Negro leadership (or the lack of it). A striking proof that no solution has been found is the fact that as late as 1964, Harlem and other Northern communities were still spawning riots.

Countee found that his writing and teaching grew more compatible as time went on. In December, 1935, he was the subject of the lead article in the Poetry Corner of *Scholastic*, a magazine for high school students. The article was illustrated with his portrait. The same issue contained excerpts from "Three Nonsense Rhymes for My Three Goddaughters" and the more serious "Any Human to Another." The latter poem stressed the interdependence of people and their need to share both joy and sorrow. He said in part:

> Let no man be so proud
> And confident
> To think he is allowed
> A little tent

154

> Pitched in a meadow
> Of sun and shadow
> All his own.

This poem became a favorite selection in anthologies for elementary and high school students.

He was now beginning to think about writing for younger readers. So he often tried out his verses by reading them to his cousin's little girls. Their greatest enjoyment came from the stories in verse about the strange animals he invented, such as the Wakeupworld with twelve eyes arranged clockwise in his head, the Lapalake that could never get enough to drink, and the proud Snakethatwalkeduponhistail. When the children demanded to know the origin of these amusing creatures, he had a ready answer. With a straight face he told them that Christopher, his cat (whom the youngsters knew and loved), had told him a long story about these unusual beasts. They were animals whose species are lost to us because they failed to get into Noah's Ark when the world was destroyed by the great flood. Each one had missed the boat because of a particular flaw in his character. Christopher had learned the story from his father through a long line of ancestors descended from the first Christopher, who had sailed on the Ark.

These stories in verse with prose interludes were later published as *The Lost Zoo*. Meanwhile Countee again became involved with a theatrical production. In Moylan, Pennsylvania, the Hedgerow Theater, a repertory company, had expressed interest in presenting a dramatic version of *One Way to Heaven*. So Countee arranged the story as a play in ten scenes. The opening production was so successful that the company decided to include the play in its repertory.

The following year was an important one for Countee Cullen, although he might not have realized it at the time. One day he ran into his friend Harry Roberson, who insisted that Countee come home with him. At the apartment they were greeted by a young woman whom Countee recognized with delight. She was Harry's sister, Ida Mae. Countee had not seen her since their meeting at The Dark Tower party seven years earlier. This year she had moved to New York.

He now had an incentive for visiting the Robersons more regularly. Ida was a pleasant hostess with the knack of making him feel comfortably at home in a casual, quiet way. Her business training seemed to give her a sense of orderliness that he admired. And he enjoyed her conversation because she liked the art world too, and she had a special interest in African art and culture.

On June 27, 1938, the citizens of Harlem suffered a great shock. In their morning newspapers they read that James Weldon Johnson had died the night before in an automobile accident. With his wife, the Negro leader had been returning from a weekend at their summer home in Maine. The crash had occurred at a railroad crossing. Mrs. Johnson had been critically injured.

Friends of both races looked back with astonishment on the long career of this versatile man. In 1901, he had come to New York already a member of the bar in Jacksonville,

Florida, where he was born. This in itself was an accomplishment for a Negro. But in New York he teamed with his brother, a musician, to compose popular songs for Broadway shows. Their success might be measured by the fact that one of their compositions brought them $13,000 in royalties, a considerable amount in those days.

James Weldon Johnson wrote serious poetry and prose too. And he made an intensive study of literature and of the origins of Negro culture. His accomplishments in these areas led to his appointment as Professor of Creative Literature at Fisk and later to a similar position at New York University.

As a champion of Negro rights Johnson had been active in founding the National Association for the Advancement of Colored People, eventually becoming its chief executive. And he had been both a forerunner and an active participant in the Negro Renaissance. Now he was dead at the age of sixty-seven.

No one was more affected by the news than Carl Van Vechten. He decided to establish at Yale University a James Weldon Johnson Memorial Collection of Negro arts and letters. Van Vechten had acquired hundreds of books, letters, and original manuscripts by and about Negroes. By 1938, he had abandoned his own writing career, taking up photography instead. Soon his collection of photographs grew to include practically every Negro in the arts, and eventually he had hundreds of these pictures to send to Yale. Then he began to solicit material from his friends.

Countee Cullen felt honored to be invited to make a contribution to this project. He searched among his keepsakes for appropriate poems, letters, and other memorabilia. Among the things he found were his treasured French notebook filled with exercises and poems; original manuscripts of "Scottsboro," "After a Visit," and his as yet unpublished "Negro Mother's Lullaby"; and letters from Yolande. He searched his mind, too, for evidence of his right to be included in the James Weldon Johnson Collection. Sometimes he wondered about his obligations as a Negro and whether he was doing all he could to fulfill them.

A year or two later these doubts were revived by an interview he had granted to a bright teen-ager named James Baldwin. This young man, a student at De Witt Clinton High School, was on the staff of *The Magpie* at the time when an anniversary number of the magazine was being prepared. The boys were working hard to get ideas for interesting features. Suddenly Mrs. Whalen, their faculty advisor, came up with one. She assigned Baldwin, an aspiring writer, to interview a Clinton alumnus who had won recognition as a poet. Thus Countee Cullen met James Baldwin.

It was a meeting of different generations and different points of view. Afterward Cullen was somewhat shocked to recognize the gap between his own conservatism and the younger man's impatience. But further reflection convinced him that the posture he had held throughout his career was an appropriate one for him. Of course, he was aware of white injustices to Negroes, and he was sensitive enough to feel deep sorrow because of this. But in his poetry he tried to show that the agony of his people was in itself a sort of spiritual triumph. Perhaps this attitude was a combination of his Methodist heritage and his poetic inclination.

CHAPTER
XIV

The spring rain made a pleasant sound as the wind slanted it across the roof and drove it in misty gusts along the yard. The water nearly hid the pointed green blades that would soon grow up to be beds of red and white and yellow tulips. It flowed over the tidy lawn and ran like a river down Grand View Boulevard in the little town of Tuckahoe, New York.

Countee Cullen tried to shake some of the water from his coat before he unlocked the door of his attractive suburban home. He had to hold tight to the doorknob to keep the wind from yanking it out of his hand. Inside he called to his wife, Ida. After his wet embrace they both burst into laughter at the sight of him as he stood there holding a silver umbrella handle. The wind had lifted away the metal ribs with their black cloth covering. He had watched the wreckage soar above his head and collapse in the distance like a huge wet bat. And now here he stood foolishly gripping the handle of what had once been a cherished souvenir from Europe while beads of water glistened on his happy face.

Ida knew that Countee was passionately fond of rain. So she had not been surprised when he dashed from the house in the middle of a storm. In fact, she had learned many things about this author and teacher since the day her brother, Harry Roberson, had first brought him to their home. While many people thought of him as serious, Ida had soon found out that Countee liked to have fun. That was why she liked Renan's painting of him in what she called his "poker clothes."

Their courtship had been filled with little pleasantries like his teaching her to play belotte. At first she thought she would never learn this complicated French card game. But his teasing and coaching finally enabled her to win sometimes. And when she won she knew she had done so on her own merit. Countee's integrity extended, she found, even to a card game. She did not believe he would have found it possible to tell a lie under any circumstances. And he stood by a principle. If you owed him five cents he wanted it when due, even if you turned around and borrowed five dollars.

Countee, in turn, had found Ida refreshingly different from many of the young women he had known. Having come from a large family she was unspoiled and considerate. And he was flattered by her sincere interest in his writing and her willingness to spend much time during their courtship listening as he read from his current manuscript. He was working at the time on *The Lost Zoo* and was pleased to discover that Ida did not think him insane when he declared that the story was being dictated to him by his cat.

Ida and Countee were married in September, 1940. They lived in a New York apartment before acquiring their home in Tuckahoe, a pretty little town in Westchester County. They both loved the country, and the location was within commuting distance of Countee's teaching job. On weekends and holidays they enjoyed planting seeds and bulbs or raking leaves, according to the season. This house was a place to acquire pleasant memories. Countee and Ida liked to entertain their friends informally with small dinners. On these occasions Ida met some of the friends, both white and colored, whom Countee had known abroad. And the lucky guests were impressed by Ida's calm, charming manner and Countee's ease in performing the duties of a good host.

One bright fall morning Countee left early for school. He boarded the New York Central commuter train at the little Tuckahoe station. The train sped merrily past the neatly hedged towns of Bronxville, Fleetwood, and Mount Vernon, past the beautiful Woodlawn Cemetery. Countee noted the contrast between these scenic places and the cheerless tenements they passed as they entered East Harlem. The elevated tracks were so close to the buildings that he could almost reach out and touch the dingy washes hung out on the fire escapes. Soon the train rumbled to a stop alongside the ancient trembling platform of the 125th Street station.

During the twenty-minute ride he previewed the day's

activities. It was to be a very special day. He had received permission to organize for a limited number of boys a class in creative writing to take the place of regular ninth-grade English. He had announced his first poetry contest, and today the boys would read their entries.

The paved schoolyard was swarming with students when he arrived. Many of them had come this morning from walk-up flats too small to house them, their parents, their brothers and sisters, and the lodgers who helped to pay the rent. There was much raucous shouting. A big boy let out some profanity, and a couple of his pals poked him vigorously in the ribs and nodded in the direction of their approaching teacher. Mr. Cullen pretended not to notice.

In the classroom there was a shuffling of feet as some of the larger boys struggled to fit their gangling legs under the junior high school desks. Cullen called the class to order and asked to see the hands of those who had written poems for the contest. In the ominous quiet the teacher scanned the solemn brown faces before him. He hoped the sinking feeling in his stomach did not show in his face. After what seemed an eternity a timid hand went up.

Before the lone volunteer was permitted to read his poem, the teacher looked it over and asked the boy to cross his heart and swear that the work was really his own. Harold was pleased to think that the verses were so fine that Mr. Cullen could doubt his ability to produce them.

The lines he read had been written as a tribute to his mother. In them the young author expressed his gratitude

163

for the sacrifices this hardworking woman had made for him, such as washing and ironing his shirts, cooking his favorite food, and giving him fifteen cents for a movie.

The unpolished lines had eloquence. As his classmates applauded, Harold took his seat and self-consciously rubbed from his sleeve a smudge of dirt left there from an early morning fight on the way to school.

Now that Harold had broken the ice, other members of the class were encouraged to read their poems. So there was a succession of homely verses delivered in shy, changing voices by Charles and Arthur and Leonardis. The winner was decided by majority vote. The prize of fifty cents was provided by the teacher.

At the end of this day Countee Cullen welcomed the ringing of the dismissal bell. He began at once to clear his desk and stack papers he would take home to correct that night. Suddenly he was aware of the figure of a boy hesitating in the doorway. It was Archie, one of his pupils.

Archie's problem was timidity. He had not volunteered to read a poem in class. But now he took from his bulging notebook the poem he considered his best and handed it to Mr. Cullen, who promised to evaluate it that night and bring him a verdict the next day.

True to his word, Cullen was ready for the after-school session. He praised Archie's work, and as a surprise he handed the boy a special award. Archie could tell by the shape of the package that the prize was a book. He thought perhaps it might be a volume of Shakespeare. Or maybe it was the poetry of Keats, that apostle of beauty Mr. Cullen was always talking about.

Excitedly he unwrapped the parcel and read the title: *The Lost Zoo* by Christopher Cat and Countee Cullen. He did not know whether to be disappointed or elated. Certainly he was surprised. The guy had never told them he was an author.

Countee had dedicated this book to the children he had taught. After its publication he received one day a batch of important critical reviews. They came from some fourth-grade pupils in a New York elementary school. Their teacher, Miss Lucile Armistead, had read them excerpts from *The Lost Zoo*, and the children were outspoken in their comments. Some of them had named their favorite animals from the book. But nearly all of them wanted to know if Christopher could really talk.

Christopher was indeed no ordinary cat. At the age of ten he was large and golden. He seemed to enjoy upstaging his younger sister, Christobelle, who was smaller and calico. He had caused Christobelle to feel so inferior that she would run and hide under a bed whenever guests admired her brother's beautiful coat.

Christopher treated his master as an equal; any chair that was good enough for Cullen was good enough for his cat. This spirit of comradeship inspired Cullen to believe there was a story to be extracted from his pet. From this inspiration, with encouragement from Countee's little goddaughters, *The Lost Zoo* was born. The love for his pets and his deep feeling for all animals gave this book a special place in Countee's affection. And he could only hope that someday Archie would know how a writer felt when he put a part of himself, a part of his life, into a book.

The conference with Archie had been one of the rewards of teaching. Countee found that these advantages overshadowed the inconveniences of his work. Of course, he regretted the time that the interminable marking of papers took away from his companionship with Ida. But he was lucky to have such an understanding wife. She knew, as he did, that the high standards of excellence he held for his pupils demanded conscientious attention to their papers.

In his way he was trying to be an "apostle of beauty" to these youngsters. He wanted to help them understand good poetry, and to this end he encouraged their interest in writing by forming a club that lasted for years after they left the junior high school.

Even while they were still in the ninth grade, one of his classes made a gesture that Cullen cherished deeply. Once while he was ill and absent for two weeks, they sent him a booklet of carefully written verses. Countee smiled as he read these words on the cover: "Poems to Our Teacher, from 9B2. This is our best."

Mentioning this touching incident later in a magazine article, Cullen admitted that the booklet did not contain great literature. "But," he said, "every one of them had bitten his pencil and written a poem. That was the point."

Times were changing now for Negro writers. For Countee the change was closely tied to his teaching career. He was writing articles for educational magazines, and his poetry was appearing in such periodicals, too. For example, there were his contributions to *Scholastic*. In addition, *The Journal* of the National Education Association used his poetry in a unique way. Their issue of December, 1941, featured a page of recent verse for children. With an introductory comment on the fresh childlike view that poets sometimes have of the world, the editor presented seven poems. One of these was "The-Snake-that-Walked-Upon-His-Tail" from Cullen's *Lost Zoo*. Among the other poets represented were Elizabeth Madox Roberts with her "Evening Hymn," and Rosemary and Stephen Vincent Benet, authors of "Nancy Hanks."

A year and a half later, in May, 1943, Cullen was again published in *The Journal*. This time the feature was a page of selections recommended for memorization by ninth-grade pupils. Once more Countee was in distinguished company. Just below the First Psalm, his poem "Simon the Cyrenian Speaks" appeared. There were also quotations from Shakespeare's *Othello* and *Julius Caesar*, "Fog," by Carl Sandburg, selections from Van Dyke, Edwin Markham, Emerson, and Lowell.

But Cullen was not competing with the Negro writers of the day. Some critics said that the colored author was now coming of age. Gone were the days of the 1920's and early 1930's when the talented few were carefully nurtured by their Negro elders and sponsored by solicitous white patrons. The opening that had been wedged during the Renaissance period was widening to admit greater numbers of courageous voices. Many Renaissance figures were still writing, among them Langston Hughes, Zora Neale Hurston, Arna Bontemps, Wallace Thurman, and Sterling Brown. But new names were appearing in the fields of both prose and poetry.

Down at Wiley College in Texas, Melvin B. Tolson, a

professor of English and speech, was winning prizes for his poems. One of these, "Dark Symphony," appeared in the *Atlantic Monthly.* Tolson also wrote plays and a newspaper column and went on to publish a volume of poems, *Rendezvous with America,* in 1944.

In 1940, Robert Hayden's book of poems, *Heart-Shaped in the Dust,* was published. Hayden, also a professor of English, later received a poetry award and Rosenwald and Ford Foundation grants. Another Rosenwald fellow, Frank Marshall Davis, had been making progress with his poetry and by 1937 had put out his second book of verse, *I Am the American Negro.* At the same time, Owen Dodson was experimenting with poetic drama. Most of the verse of this era was vigorous and unrestrained in its protest against the Negro's lot in America.

The novelists of the 1940's were even more outspoken. The most spectacular among them was Richard Wright. His *Native Son,* appearing in 1940, hit the literary world with force. Critics praised Wright's artistic skill, his incisive style, and his ability to analyze the social influences that affected the underprivileged Negro. Many readers resented the sensational aspects of the novel, the violence of deed and language. But no one could deny that the talented author had made an original contribution to the growing body of fiction written by Negroes.

Wright had turned away from the vogue of the 1920's and 1930's that sought to focus attention on the middle class Negro. It is understandable that the Renaissance writers should want to present to the reading public a less stereotyped image than the ignorant buffoon of earlier days. But Wright was interested in the masses. He wanted to show the struggles of the vast majority of black people rather than to exalt the few who were more fortunate.

Other novelists, though not so phenomenally successful as Wright, departed from tradition each in his own way. William Attaway used white characters in *Let Me Breathe Thunder*, and Frank Yerby wrote historical novels without regard for race.

It was obvious to Countee Cullen that the Negro writer was entering a new era. He could see the dawning of the day he had long hoped for when the work of his contemporaries and that of future writers would be judged by literary standards with no allowances made for the fact that they were Negroes.

His own ambitions were now pointed toward writing more plays. But his bouts with illness were becoming more frequent. Countee had never been a complainer, and he did not want to worry his wife and his father. But in a letter to a friend he confided that he was constantly plagued with headaches. His illness was diagnosed as hypertension. The medical profession believed that this extremely high blood pressure was related to kidney failure. But his physician did not discount the nervous and emotional factors involved, so he advised Culleen against driving himself to the point of exhaustion. Countee gave a wry smile at the thought of a teacher taking it easy. Short of resigning his position there was no way to keep from being emotionally keyed up.

So he kept on studying and seeking fresh and interesting ways to present material to his classes. And he continued to do extra things to help his culturally deprived students.

One of his projects was an annual Christmas party for the boys. He always invited them to his home for the occasion. Preparations for these parties could not have been more carefully made if Cullen had expected a head of state. The boys were exposed to a fine example of gracious living. But they had fun, too, enjoying the original games, good music, and the delicious and interesting foods their teacher provided.

Added to the pressures of his schoolwork was Countee's feeling of urgency in getting ahead with his writing. He wanted to finish another "Christopher" book. Then he would concentrate on writing for the theater. Already he had received an offer from Remo Bufano and Mura Dehn to collaborate on a dramatic ballet based on *The Lost Zoo*. And he was still hoping to write the libretto for an opera. Meanwhile he continued to compose poems, writing them out carefully by hand (he could never compose at the typewriter) and going over them again, revising and polishing.

He worried, too, about the war. He was resigned to the fact that his yearly trips to France had been curtailed; this was only a personal inconvenience. But he was deeply concerned over the world situation. And the combination of problems was not good for his ulcer nor for the persistent headaches.

CHAPTER

XV

On a tuesday evening in 1943, Countee was hurrying to the Forty-fourth Street Theater. From Times Square he made his way west and headed for the basement of the playhouse. He was late and the Stage Door Canteen was already in operation. The large room was alive with military personnel. They represented most of the countries opposing the Axis Powers. Every night of the week, between the hours of five and midnight, nearly two thousand of them showed up.

Men and women on leave were happy to spend their free evening hours in this place. There was no alcohol, just food and fun. There was no charge; the price of admission was simply the wearing of a uniform. This was good, for no G.I. could have afforded to pay for the caliber of service dispensed here. Professionals from the world of entertainment and the literary arts ran the canteen. It was a routine matter to find Alfred Lunt and Tallulah

Bankhead washing dishes, and Hazel Scott or Shirley Booth performing on their regularly assigned nights.

Countee played his usual game of trying to identify the various uniforms as he moved toward his station near the kitchen. On Tuesday nights he was a waiter assigned to Captain Carl Van Vechten. Sometimes Brock Pemberton was one of their bus boys. Cullen's experience as a waiter in Atlantic City during a college vacation was helpful to him now. He handled his tray like a veteran as he moved from table to table with a friendly smile. His boss, Mr. Van Vechten, liked to joke about the pleasure he derived from giving orders to a Harvard man.

The volunteers enjoyed this sort of banter. In fact, they sometimes had even more fun than the guests. But they all prided themselves on the efficiency with which they performed their chores, agreeing that they should spare no pains in giving these service men and women the best that Broadway had to offer.

Countee was grateful to be a part of this war effort. Back in 1935, Harlem's reaction to the invasion of Ethiopia had alerted him to the growing unrest in the world. Then with a heavy heart he had learned in June, 1940, of the fall of France. In December of the following year the United States formally declared war on Japan after the infamous Pearl Harbor attack. By this time Countee was thirty-eight years old, and he knew that his age and physical condition would make active military service unlikely for him.

He tried not to think of his health now, even though he seemed to be gradually falling apart. Once in Paris he had told a friend laughingly that he was annoyed with the doctor who had discovered his ulcer because the diagnosis interfered with his enjoyment of rich French cooking. And now the hypertensive headaches kept bothering him.

Countee ignored these attacks as much as possible because of the many things he wanted to do. First of all, he felt his responsibility for regular attendance at his teaching post. He was reluctant, too, to miss his Tuesday night duties at the Stage Door Canteen. And then he still loved going to the theater.

Whenever they had tickets for a Broadway show, he was a bundle of nervous energy. He helped Ida with the kitchen chores so that they would not be late. Nothing must prevent their arriving in plenty of time to find their seats and enjoy the enchanted moment when the lights go down and the curtain starts to rise. Then Countee's feeling of expectation rose to its full height. And he brought this enthusiasm to every kind of theatrical performance—the opera, the symphony, a recital, a jazz program, an O'Neill play, or the Katherine Dunham Dancers.

Since World War II had forced Countee to discontinue his annual trips to Europe (his last visit was made in 1938), he and Ida spent their summers in the country. They chose resort spots where they could quietly enjoy the out-of-doors: the old place in Pleasantville, or scenic Lake Placid, or a beach in Maine. Countee found these places convenient for writing, and the pleasant country nights formed a romantic background for reading to his one-woman audience.

After the success of *The Lost Zoo*, Cullen decided to

173

let Christopher write his autobiography under the title *My Lives and How I Lost Them*. As everyone knows, all cats have nine lives. The collaborators thought their readers would like to learn how Christopher, who was now in his ninth life, had lost the other eight. The tales turned out to be full of adventure and humor with some canny observations on the foibles of humans as well. Instead of the fanciful colored illustrations that Charles Sebree had contributed to *The Lost Zoo*, *My Lives* featured whimsical black and white drawings by Robert Reid Macguire.

When the book was published in 1942, the jacket contained a hearty endorsement by Carl Van Vechten. This author, now turned photographer, had also taken the picture of Cullen that appeared on the back flap. The two men had gone to a spot near the zoo in Central Park. Here Countee posed sitting on a park bench. The strongly patterned bark of a stately tree served as a background for his serious face. He wore a well-tailored gray suit, a white shirt, and a figured tie that seemed to repeat the pattern of the tree's bark. Obviously Cullen still held the high regard for pictures and books that he had shown on that day long ago when, at the age of eleven, he had posed with his favorite storybook.

The photograph for *My Lives* was a fine, sensitive likeness. It was one of hundreds of pictures that Van Vechten made for his growing collection of Negroes in the arts that eventually made their way to the James Weldon Johnson display at the Yale Library.

After he had finished his latest book, Countee found a little more time for community service. He was often called upon to lend his voice to the causes of race relations and civil rights.

A case in point was the disturbance in Hillburn, New York. By the fall of 1943, the trouble stirred up by the Harlem riot of August 1 seemed to have spilled over into Hillburn. This small community of little more than a thousand citizens was located in Rockland County very near the New Jersey state line and not far from New York City. Many Harlemites who heard of the situation were quick to blame the influence of New Jersey, a state they sarcastically referred to as the Georgia of the North.

In October, a man named Malcolm Stead was accused of inciting the people of Hillburn to racial hatred. Sixty-three Negro and white mothers organized a protest march. Their effort inspired other residents to form a Rockland County Citizens Committee to investigate reported incidents of violence and discrimination.

On October 20, the committee held a meeting. A feature of the program was a poem by Cullen written for the occasion and set to music by a composer named Waldemar Hille. Titled "Hillburn the Fair," the lyrics began, "God have pity/ On such a city/ Where parent teaches child to hate." The following week in *The People's Voice,* a local newspaper, Cullen's poem appeared. It had become a battle cry for democracy in Hillburn.

But community work was an extracurricular activity for Countee. Teaching was still an ever present concern, as he realized one day early in 1944. He was going over his plan book, putting the finishing touches on the units for 9A English and 9B French, when he came across his

175

rating report from the Board of Education. He had hidden it between the leaves of the book for future filing. He was delighted to read again the special notation that his principal, George Zuckerman, had written. It contained a compliment to Cullen's work at the school and to his fine personality. And Mr. Zuckerman had expressed the hope that Countee would decide to stay at 139. This was one of the bright moments of his career as a teacher.

But many of the bright spots of his career as an author were now coming from recognition of pieces he had already published. He could now read his poems in several of the established anthologies, including *Great Poems of the English Language* (Tudor, 1937), *Modern American Poetry* (Harcourt, Brace, 1942), and *The Democratic Spirit* (Knopf, 1941).

Yet he had not spent all of his lyrical power. Essentially a poet, he found that for him the muse touched every experience. In November, 1943, while he was hospitalized for a tonsillectomy he penned "Lines for a Hospital." Later he sent the poem to Carl Van Vechten for the Yale collection. In an accompanying letter he said he had written the lines between hemorrhages. "Ye blind, ye deaf, ye mute!" it began, "Ho, here's healing!"

Earlier the words of Gandhi, "Karenge ya Marenge" (Do or die), had inspired him to write a poem comparing the Indian leader's cry to Patrick Henry's famous line about liberty. And he was moved to regret that the world was paying too little attention to Gandhi's idealism.

Finally in July, 1944, the plight of France became the theme of a poem titled "La Belle, La Douce, La Grande."

Cullen said that loveliness and gentleness and greatness would come to France again, for, he predicted, the mantle of Joan of Arc falling on Charles De Gaulle would invest him with the power to restore his country to its rightful place in a free world. The very next month Paris was liberated. On the twenty-fifth of August, 1944, the Allied armies entered the city as the bells of Notre Dame tolled in welcome. And Countee, heart's brother of the French, rejoiced when he heard the news.

In the 1940's, Cullen was still accepting engagements to lecture and read his poetry. Although he still had momentary stagefright on these occasions, he loved the contacts with people. He had the opportunity to meet audiences of many kinds. He was always at home on college campuses, both at the large universities and at the smaller schools such as Western, a women's college in Oxford, Ohio, where he was the first Negro poet most of the students had ever seen. He was equally familiar with church audiences like the group he read to in August, 1945, at the Twenty-eighth Street Christian Church in Los Angeles.

On September 27, 1945, Countee Cullen wrote an important letter. It was addressed to Miss Amy Flashner, an editor at Harper and Brothers. In it he discussed plans for a book of poems to be selected from his previous volumes. He said that since he did not intend to publish another book of verse, this volume should represent the best of his life's work. With the letter he included a list of the poems he would like to see in such a collection.

Cullen had a good basis for judging the lasting value of his verse—the reaction of his public. Whenever a person whose opinion he respected had something good to say about a poem, he was encouraged to believe in its worth. For example, Mrs. Roosevelt's enthusiasm for "The Black Christ" convinced him that, despite its length, it should be included in the new book.

Another factor that influenced his choice was the response of his listeners. As he gave readings in churches, lecture rooms, and homes in all parts of the country, he was keenly alert to audience reactions. The pattern did not vary much from New York to Indianapolis to Los Angeles. He made a mental note when he saw a smile of recognition for the subtle humor in an epitaph. He learned to measure the intensity of applause. And he was moved by the requests of those who wished to buy some of his books that were out of print. As he told Miss Flashner, he did not think he should include in his anthology selections from *The Lost Zoo* because he believed people would still buy this book if it were reissued.

Cullen reviewed his six books of poetry with care now. It was like living his whole life over again to reread the lines and recall the circumstances under which they had been written. Some of the memories were happy and some were painful, but all were welcome. Slowly he added titles to his list until at last he had chosen the eighty-nine selections on which he would stake his reputation as a poet. The list included twenty-five selections from *Color*, twenty-one from *Copper Sun*, twenty-four from *The Black Christ* (including the title poem), eighteen from *The*

178

Medea, and the entire *Ballad of The Brown Girl.* Later he added six poems previously unpublished.

"Christus Natus Est." Countee thought of the words he had written and of the musical setting Charles Howard Marsh had composed for them. The Iowa-born organist and choirmaster had woven a choral work around the eight stanzas that Cullen had written at Christmas time in 1943. Depicting the sufferings of mankind and especially the senseless carnage of war, the poem points out the redemptive purpose of the birth of Christ:

> The manger still
> Outshines the throne;
> Christ must and will
> Come to his own.
> Hosannah!   Christus natus est.

Countee remembered the Christmas of 1943 when the world was still at war. He remembered, too, other poems of his that had been set to music. Marsh had previously composed melodies for four of Cullen's epitaphs and for the sweetly lyrical "If You Should Go." This poem had appeared in his first book, *Color.* Consisting of only two stanzas, it ran:

> Love, leave me like the light,
>   The gently passing day;
> We would not know, but for the night,
>   When it has slipped away.
>
> Go quietly; a dream
>   When done, should leave no trace

179

That it has lived, except a gleam
Across the dreamer's face.

These same lines attracted the attention of another composer, William Grant Still, who created a musical setting for them. Still's career was an inspiration to the Renaissance and the post-Renaissance Negro. Even in the early thirties he was composing and arranging music for motion pictures, radio, and the theater. And in 1936, he conducted a major symphony orchestra in the Hollywood Bowl.

Countee was happy to have had yet another poem associated with famous musicians. In April, 1943, he had written "Dear Friends and Gentle Hearts," a tribute to the friendships that enhance our lives from birth to death. William Lawrence, a composer and arranger long associated with some of the top Negro singers, wrote music for these lyrics and the song was later sung by the great Marian Anderson.

Now it was Christmas 1945. Propped up in the spacious living room of his Tuckahoe home Countee Cullen closed his eyes and listened to the deep resonant voice of his brother-in-law, Orlando Roberson, the concert singer. At the baby grand piano Ida played a soft accompaniment to the familiar carols. Countee smiled as he marked the rhythm of the tunes with his fingers while Christopher purred nearby. Of all the songs connected with the church, Christmas music was his favorite. This year he was too ill to attend the holiday services. His hypertensive condition had worsened to the point where he was forced

180

to obey the doctor's orders to go to bed. So Ida and Orlando had brought the music to him. His face shone with gratitude.

It was strange to spend the holidays so quietly. He missed the busy streets with the crowds of shoppers jostling and pushing each other in and out of stores. He remembered the rosy cheeks of the chestnut vendor stationed near the Fifth Avenue library with his knitted cap pulled down over his ears. This jolly fellow always had a cheery word for the customers who waited patiently while he warmed his chapped hands over the little stove before handing out the tiny bags of shiny brown roasted chestnuts. Countee could visualize, too, the long lines of people waiting to see the special Christmas show at Radio City Music Hall. He thought of the holiday concerts and of the Broadway matinees lively with the chatter of students on vacation.

A flash of memory took him back to his early years at Junior High School 139 when, after watch meeting, he and his young teacher friends would drop by the Roberts' home for a lucky dish of black-eyed peas. This year he was grounded. But he had much to be thankful for. Here he was surrounded by love and comfort. Pa, who had retired from Salem because of ill health, was living with the younger Cullens, and Ida was as attentive to the old man as if he had been her own father. On the preceding Friday, the last day before Christmas vacation, he had provided the annual Christmas party for the boys in his classes at 139. Countee was glad that his illness had not forced him to disappoint them.

181

It was to be Cullen's last Christmas. On New Year's Day his discomfort began to increase, and soon the pain was almost unbearable. The hastily summoned physician rushed him to Sydenham Hospital where he remained under treatment for a few days. Then on the morning of January 10, 1946, thousands of people opened their newspapers to be stunned by the simple headline, "Countee Cullen, Negro Poet, Dead." The report listed the cause of his death as uremic poisoning.

The New York press devoted several columns to the news of Cullen's passing. The *Times* traced his career from the De Witt Clinton days when he won his first prize for, "I Have a Rendezvous with Life," to the publication of his last book, *My Lives and How I Lost them.* His honors and awards were recounted there: the three Witter Bynner prizes, the John Reed Memorial award, his election to Phi Beta Kappa, the Harmon award, the Amy Spingarn prize, and the Guggenheim fellowship. There were quotations from his poems and references to his lyrical brilliance.

Once more Salem Methodist Episcopal Church stood as a symbol in Cullen's career. Three thousand people attended his funeral services there on Saturday the twelfth of January as the rain cleared and the day grew colder. There were boys he had taught and church members who had known him from childhood. Actors, writers, and men in public life came to pay a final tribute. Richard Wright attended, and so did William Stanley Braithwaite, Rex Ingram, Canada Lee, Judge Hubert Delany, and Ridgely

Torrence. And his old friends Arna Bontemps, Alain Locke, and Carl Van Vechten were there.

The Reverend Charles Trigg, who had succeeded Dr. Cullen as Salem's pastor, spoke simply of Countee's loyalty, devoutness, and respect for humanity. Principal George Zuckerman praised Cullen's work as a teacher. Roy DeCoverly paid the tribute from one poet to another.

Two items of unfinished business were completed after his death. *St. Louis Woman* opened on Broadway in April. And early in 1947, *On These I Stand* was published. It was the book Countee Cullen had outlined to Amy Flashner in the last year of his life.

CHAPTER
XVI

"S T. LOUIS WOMAN" went into rehearsal around the middle of January, 1946. On Saturday, March 30, it opened at the Martin Beck Theatre. Billed as a musical play, it had many features of the earlier Negro musicals with the addition of a plot. The dancing Nicholas brothers were in the cast, Harold starring as Little Augie, and Fayard playing a lesser role. Ruby Hill, an experienced singer and actress was the St. Louis Woman, while Pearl Bailey made her Broadway debut as a character known as Butterfly.

Negro theatergoers recognized other names in the cast. Rex Ingram had appeared in motion pictures and on the stage. Juanita Hall of the Hall-Johnson Choir was later to be featured as Bloody Mary in the stage and movie versions of *South Pacific*.

With the music of Harold Arlen, the lyrics of Johnny Mercer, and the direction of Rouben Mamoulian added to the talented cast, the play seemed to have every advantage necessary for a long run. But it closed on Saturday, July 6, one of many Broadway shows to succumb during the hot summer of 1946.

The year had been one in which Negro themes had flourished on the stage. Some of the shows running at the same time as *St. Louis Woman* were *Anna Lucasta,* a drama of Negro life, at the Mansfield Theatre on Forty-seventh Street; *Carmen Jones,* Oscar Hammerstein's fast-moving version of Bizet's opera featuring an all-Negro cast, at the New York City Center; *Show Boat* at the Zeigfeld Theatre; and *Deep Are the Roots,* a problem play, at the Fulton Theatre on Forty-sixth Street. These four productions, unlike *St. Louis Woman,* were written by white authors.

During the same summer Cullen's name again appeared in connection with a play. The August issue of *Theatre Arts* magazine contained the text of "The Third Fourth of July," a one-act play in poetry by Owen Dodson and Countee Cullen. Dodson, in addition to being a poet, was a serious student of the drama and became a director of the Howard University Players. An ardent believer in the worth of the Negro college theater, he later saw his own plays produced by student groups.

"The Third Fourth of July" deals with the way the second World War touched the lives of two families, one white and one Negro. Designed so that the activities of both families might be seen on stage at the same time, their homes are separated only by a wall. Symbolically the characters wear masks whenever black meets white. Introduced by two narrators (one black, one white) speaking in verse, the action is carried out through the singing and dancing of the characters. When a son-in-law of the Negro family is killed in the war, the message is delivered by mistake to the white family's home. This circumstance establishes a line of communication between the two households. When the fortunate parents whose son has returned unharmed deliver the sad message, the Negro family's grief proves powerful enough to cause both groups to remove their masks. With appropriate songs and dances all join to celebrate the "third fourth of July."

This play with its subtle implications received little notice at a time when Negro writers were lifting angry voices in a direct and militant manner. Moreover, Harlem was beginning to be known as a decaying slum area. Yet even in the same month (August, 1946) when Cullen and Dodson's play appeared, *The New York Times Magazine* published an article in defense of the Negro community. Titled "The Other and Unknown Harlem," the piece was authored by the distinguished novelist Fannie Hurst. She based her story on visits she had made to respectable middle class families in a clean, quiet neighborhood north of 145th Street. She described two such households. One was the home of a chiropodist and his family. The other belonged to Bouchet Day, a teacher whose wife was a daughter of Fred Moore, owner and editor of the *New York Age*. Moore had bought the paper back in 1907 and had guided it through years of Republican conservatism until his death.

In the week following the publication of Miss Hurst's article many readers wrote in their reactions. Most of the

186

letters that appeared in the paper a week later voiced the agreement of members of both races with the author's point of view. Some of the letter writers added personal experiences to emphasize the fact that all Negroes were indeed not necessarily primitive and exotic, nor rebellious and dirty.

In intellectual circles the middle class Negro continued to advance. An example of this progress was New York University's appointment of its first full-time Negro professor. He was Dr. Ira DeA. Reid, who in the fall of 1946 left his post as chairman of the sociology department at Atlanta University to take the job at NYU. Appointed as a visiting professor, he taught a full schedule in the School of Education, specializing in Negro culture and education.

James Weldon Johnson had broken the ice at NYU in 1934 when he began teaching special courses in racial contributions, and he continued to do so until his death. Now, eight years later, Reid was receiving his appointment. He had been born in Virginia and was educated at Atlanta University, the University of Pittsburgh, and finally at Columbia where he received the Ph.D. degree. He also studied at the London School of Economics.

By February, 1947, when Cullen's *On These I Stand* was published posthumously, the social center of Harlem had begun to move northward. On Edgecombe Avenue at 155th Street stood a handsome apartment building. It had been bought from its white owners by a group of West Indian realtors and was commonly known to Harlemites simply by the number of its address, 409. The promontory on which it stood had been nicknamed Sugar Hill, a designation that now replaced Strivers' Row, the former symbol of Negro affluence. From the Hill its residents could look down (literally and figuratively) on the aging residences and crowded tenements of lower Harlem.

Some of the Negro elite had moved, like the Cullens, to the suburbs in Westchester County or out to Long Island. But many celebrities chose the elegant convenience of 409 or a similar structure at 555 Edgecombe Avenue. The directories in the lobbies of these two buildings read like a Negro "Who's Who": Walter White of the NAACP and Lester Granger of the National Urban League; Aaron Douglas, the artist; Josh White, the ballad singer; Langston Hughes, DuBois, and physicians, dentists, lawyers, judges, and teachers.

The view from Sugar Hill was a commanding one. Apartment dwellers on the upper floors could see what was going on in the Polo Grounds behind them, or on a clear day they could sight Yankee Stadium to the east. Southward, on its own part of the hill, stood the impressive buildings of the College of the City of New York. This was the Harlem that was now the center of Negro culture much as the old Harlem had served the personalities of the Renaissance period. But now, more than a decade later, there was still no dearth of ideas or ambitions. Indeed many leaders foresaw an even greater resurgence of artistic activity with fresh young talent adding to the foundation laid by their predecessors.

Out in Chicago a young girl had been writing poems since her high school days and shyly submitting them to the *Chicago Defender,* a Negro weekly newspaper. She had been reared in Chicago by educated parents. She attended the public schools and a junior college. When her poetry came to the notice of Harlemites, the older poets were prophetic in their belief that here was a writer who would be accepted on her merit without regard to race. So in 1948, when Gwendolyn Brooks received the Pulitzer Prize in poetry, there was rejoicing in Harlem. For some of Cullen's colleagues, however, the joy was tinged with regret that Countee had not lived to see this day.

As the decade of the forties drew to a close, Harlem's intellectual leaders sensed the growing unrest of the Negro masses, and many of the "talented tenth" began to identify more closely with their less fortunate brothers. The masses could not be ignored. Many a man who had elevated himself to a place of acceptance in the white world wondered uncomfortably if a black man in Mississippi could receive the same privileges.

There were signs of increasing recognition of the need for better race relations. The list of awards to foster such improvement was steadily growing. For example, the Julian Messner award, established in 1945, was won in 1946 by Shirley Graham for her book, *There Was Once a Slave: the Heroic Story of Frederick Douglass.* In the opinion of the judges she had written the best book that year "promoting racial or religious tolerance in America."

Then in 1948, when the 1947 Honor Roll of Race Relations was announced by the curator of the Schomburg Collection of the New York Public Library, nineteen winners representing both whites and Negroes were recognized. Among the Negroes Williard Motley was cited for his best-selling novel, *Knock on Any Door*. In this book the author expressed his protest against big-city slum conditions by using poor white characters instead of Negroes. He spoke for all the masses.

Now Negro leaders were saying in public that no individual could be really free until all were free. Paul Robeson, for example, was interspersing his concert numbers with little speeches on civil rights. Middle class Negroes were embarrassed by this turn of events, much as they had been disturbed years earlier by the race-conscious preachments of Marcus Garvey. But whereas they could dismiss Garveyism as an appeal to the ignorant masses, they could not ignore Robeson so easily. He was a highly intelligent and talented man whose extreme sensitivity to the sufferings of black men had caused him (in the opinion of some) to go astray.

Again in the writings of DuBois the fate of the black man in Africa as well as in America was a primary consideration. This concern was certainly not new to DuBois. He had been devoted to the problem for half a century. He reiterated his beliefs in a book called *The World and Africa*, published in 1947. His strong indictment of the white race evoked some unfavorable comment. But the old warrior was undaunted. At the age of eighty, just before he resigned his position as research director for the NAACP, he wrote a feature article for *The New York Times* titled "The Negro Since 1900: A Progress Report." It was a calm, factual look at the conditions that had plagued him all his life.

Now that DuBois was growing older and even more impatient, his ideas on black nationalism were taking firmer root among the ordinary people. Conservative leaders, torn by mixed emotions, began to be mournfully prophetic of dangerous uprisings.

The empathy that had shown itself back in 1918 when the older Cullen had gone to Washington to plead for the condemned soldiers in Texas had never really died. The spirit of the protest marchers who had invaded New York's Fifth Avenue after the first World War was still alive. But now the malcontents were protesting not just the injustices to their Southern brothers. They were thinking of themselves. And the search for individual identity that had come alive during the Negro Renaissance had developed into a broader social movement.

The wintry beauty of the Yale University campus in New Haven, Connecticut, formed the setting for the formal opening of the James Weldon Johnson Memorial Collection of Negro Arts and Letters. The date was Saturday, January 7, 1950. The task of storing and displaying the hundreds of books, letters, manuscripts, photographs, and recordings had been completed. At last Carl Van Vechten, the donor of this material, could view his gift and receive the thanks of a grateful university.

Sterling Memorial Library, sedate in its ivy covering, made an impressive if somewhat incongruous home for the collection. From its massive wooden doors with the sturdy hardware, to its lofty upstairs rooms, this building symbolized all that was fine and enduring in American culture. Now the artistic creations of the country's largest minority group were being added to this culture.

Van Vechten had started his collection about 1924 when he was gathering material for his novel about Harlem life. In addition to the books by and about Negroes, he had acquired musical recordings—by Marian Anderson, Ethel Waters, Louis "Satchmo" Armstrong, and Edward "Duke" Ellington—that had since become rare, and in some cases totally unavailable. There were four hundred discs in the collection. And the photographs, all taken by Van Vechten himself, numbered close to a thousand. Through his sustained contacts with people who were vitally concerned with his hobby he had made this exhibit a testimony not only to his friend, James Weldon Johnson, but also to the community Johnson represented, and to the growing cosmopolitan spirit of America.

The audience at the Yale ceremony included as honored guests Van Vechten, Mrs. James Weldon Johnson, Langston Hughes, Mrs. Countee Cullen, and Levi Jackson. Jackson, a recent graduate, had captained the Yale football team and had been the first Negro so honored in Ivy League history.

Another first at these exercises was the presentation of the Bergen Lecture by a Negro. Each year an outstanding figure in the literary arts was chosen to deliver an address on the subject of his specialty. In previous years Robert Frost and T. S. Eliot had been lecturers. This year the honor went to Dr. Charles S. Johnson, president of Fisk University.

Dr. Johnson, a recognized authority on the subject, had

some interesting things to say about the place of the Negro creative artist in the stream of American culture. He entered a plea for objectivity in evaluating the Negro, and he cited Carl Van Vechten as one who exemplified true objective judgment. He spoke of the white writers who had helped to give the Negro a place of dignity and respect in American life. He pointed also to the influence of James Weldon Johnson on white Americans as well as on members of his own race. Then Yale's president, Dr. Charles Seymour, read the resolution passed by the board to commend Mr. Van Vechten and to thank him for his valuable gift.

This collection contained, among other things, the substance and spirit of the Negro Renaissance. The music of the early twenties, sometimes considered an overture to the vogue for Negro arts and letters, was represented by such diverse recordings as the blues sung by Bessie Smith, music composed and played by Duke Ellington, popular songs sung by Ethel Waters, the unique trumpet and vocal stylings of Louis Armstrong, and the inimitable voice of Marian Anderson singing both classics and spirituals.

Representative works by white authors who had sought to interpret the Negro of this era included plays by Eugene O'Neill, poetry by Vachel Lindsay, and fiction by Dubose Heyward.

From the works by Negro writers, books by Booker T. Washington were included. And although the philosophy of this early leader and educator had since been rejected by many Negro intellectuals, no one would deny that he had made a valuable contribution to the emergence of the "new" Negro. When the Harlem Renaissance began, one of its most prolific writers, Langston Hughes, contributed works in several media—poetry, novel, short story, drama —and his writings found a significant place in the Yale collection. The novels and essays of Walter White, the writings of Wallace Thurman and those of Richard Wright were only a few of the featured exhibits. And finally Countee Cullen, the lyrical voice of the Renaissance, was represented as we have seen. Again there was regret that he never saw the completed display.

In the spring following the formal opening of the James Weldon Johnson Memorial Collection, another significant event took place eight hundred miles away. In Greencastle, Indiana, on the campus of DePauw University, five hundred seniors and alumni gathered on May 26 for the presentation of the Old Gold Goblet. This award was given each year to a distinguished alumnus chose by vote of the senior class.

The recipient, Dr. Percy L. Julian, was a Negro and a chemist. In 1920, he had graduated from DePauw with Phi Beta Kappa honors. He continued his scientific education at Harvard and at the University of Vienna. Then he became noted for his work with cortisone and gained patents for several chemical discoveries. In 1950, when his alma mater tapped him for the Old Gold award, he was Director of Research and Manager of Fine Chemicals for the Glidden Company in Chicago.

Dr. Julian's address on this occasion was a stirring chal-

194

lenge to the graduates. He spoke of the condition of the world, and he advised the young people to keep their idealism. On the subject of Russia he denounced the attitude of hysteria brought on by the fear of communism. He said that this fear had caused us to adopt the negative policy of determining our actions by doing the opposite of whatever the Russians decided to do. But now, he said, we are beginning to assume a positive attitude, making decisions without respect to the beliefs of others. And it was this positive attitude that would eventually defeat communism.

He went on to discuss the state of our democracy. Dramatically he asked his audience to visualize what a "mystic historian on the planet of Mars" might write about our country one hundred years from now. Through the eyes of the Martian, Julian described the early years of America. He spoke of the idealistic words of this country's historic documents, of the stirring words of its anthems. But he noted that Americans had failed to impress the essence of these words into their hearts and souls. So the curious paradox arose that even as the Declaration of Independence was being written, its framers could hear outside the crack of the slave-driver's whip and the moan of a dying black man.

Dr. Julian's enthusiasm rose as he continued the mock historical account. He pictured the ghettos where colored children sang of "the land of the free and the home of the brave," as the visitors realized that all people were not free in this land. Then, according to Julian's fable, "a brown boy stood up and softly murmured to his fel-

low prisoners, 'Yet do I marvel at this curious thing—
to make a poet black and bid him sing!' "

The brown boy was Countee Cullen. And the speaker
quoted one of his songs:

> Once riding in old Baltimore
>   Heart-filled, head-filled with glee,
> I saw a Baltimorean
>   Keep looking straight at me.
>
> Now I was eight and very small,
>   And he was no whit bigger,
> And so I smiled, but he poked out
>   His tongue, and called me 'Nigger.'
>
> I saw the whole of Baltimore
>   From May until December;
> Of all the things that happened there
>   That's all that I remember.

Still in the framework of his fable Julian quoted the same
poem in German translation—"Ich fuhr einmal nach Baltimore"—to show how, through their interest in American
literature and culture, people all over the world have become acquainted with American prejudice.

Having completed the mythical historian's report, Percy
Julian concluded his speech with a simple plea: "When
you meet a black child, remember you have broken bread
with me and give him your hand. For on him depends the
fate of this country and of the world."

CHAPTER

XVII

Frederick asbury cullen outlived his son by six months. He had time to count his blessings. In his career as a minister he had been blessed with a cooperative and appreciative congregation. They had retired him as pastor emeritus with a gift of money and the right to live in the parsonage for his lifetime. He was blessed, too, with the privilege of following to the end the career of his adopted son whose filial devotion had always been a source of comfort.

In the months following Countee Cullen's death his friends and admirers were eager to express their awareness of the social and literary contributions he had made to their world. The New York City Board of Education paid verbal tribute to his memory, extolling his accomplishments as a teacher and a poet. Many of the magazines that had published his poems now had touching obituaries.

There were personal tributes, too. An outstanding gesture was made by Countee's close friend, Harold Jackman. At the Atlanta University Library in 1942, Jackman had established a collection of materials representative of contemporary Negro life. When Countee died, Harold moved at once to have this material named the Countee Cullen Memorial Collection.

For years Mr. Jackman had been saving items pertaining to Negro culture. He had begun with theater bills and programs. He had mementos of plays in which Negroes had roles dating back to 1926. He had also saved concert programs, newspaper reviews, magazine articles, and advertisements.

After his decision to give his personal collection to the library, Jackman began to request items from friends to add to the exhibit. The gratifying response turned up printer's proofs of books by Cullen and two other writers who, like Countee, supported themselves primarily by teaching. One, Margaret Walker, had won the Yale University competition for younger poets. The other, Horace Mann Bond, had written significant articles and books on the education of the Negro.

There were original manuscripts by Arna Bontemps, Gwendolyn Brooks, Pearl Buck, Langston Hughes, Carl Van Vechten, Walter White, and Owen Dodson. Van Vechten also gave a number of the artistic photographs of outstanding Negroes for which he had now become famous. The collection, still growing, stands as a memorial not only to the civic and artistic interests of the Negro people but also to Cullen's involvement in these activities.

In a different way there were other personal testimonies to the influence of Cullen. That of Charles Kirnon, a former student at 139, is a typical example. After his graduation from college in June, 1951, Charles went abroad on a touring fellowship. On his return he discussed his former teacher with an interviewer. He was glad to reminisce.

Memory took him back to the day they first met in junior high school when Mr. Cullen had taken over a seventh-grade class for the day. They became acquainted over a poem Charles had written. When the boy reached the ninth grade, he found that Cullen was the official teacher there. So Charles joined the creative writing group. The boys enjoyed writing last lines to their teacher's limericks and hearing him read good poetry. They wrote parodies and plays and pieces for choral speaking.

Charles remembered the day two of his own poems were presented at a choral-speaking festival at Columbia University. Mr. Cullen had made this possible. And at his teacher's urging, the boy had submitted a poem that was accepted for publication in the anthology of the National High School Poetry Association. Charles' was the only entry by a junior high school pupil to be included.

His greatest thrill came from an invitation to accompany his teacher when Cullen was a guest on the Mary Margaret McBride radio show. After the poet had read and talked, he introduced his pupil. Charles managed to keep from shaking as he read his original poem, "Prayer for Times of War." He was surprised at the kind reception the studio audience gave him. But he was even more impressed by the warmth of their greeting for Mr. Cullen.

After the program Mr. Cullen took Charles home and

visited with his mother. They talked about the boy's education and the possibilities for his future. Later Mrs. Kirnon was happy to tell people how this good man had helped her boy and other children in his classes. Specifically Charles was grateful that Mr. Cullen had made him a reader of *The New York Times*, inspired in him the urge to travel, and fired his ambition to become a writer.

Already a drive was under way to have a New York public school named for Countee Cullen. The main obstacle to the immediate accomplishment of this objective was a rule that the person to be so honored must have been dead for at least ten years. But the committee of Cullen's admirers was indefatigable. One of its most active members, Mrs. Lula B. Roache, was the widow of Frederick Cullen's nephew. She had served as a church clerk for Salem and had helped to nurse Dr. Cullen during his last illness. The patience and tireless efforts of the committee were rewarded some eighteen years after Countee's death when Public School 194 on 144th Street in Harlem became the Countee Cullen School.

Like a pebble tossed into a pond, Cullen's work was subtly spreading its influence in many directions. From London, Peter Abrahams, the South African writer, told of having first heard of Cullen in Johannesburg. And from Nigeria reports came that a Countee Cullen poetry club had been formed there.

Back in the United States, Leon Rains, a California widower, had uncovered among his late wife's papers a poem she had written:

To Countee Cullen on Reading "Color"

To you whose lips have framed in joy and grief
Sweet song a-quiver with the throb of life.
To you, young poet, who has felt the strife
And strain of bitterness and unbelief.
To you, strange prophet of a hidden store
Of melody and beauty bound
Within a race 'till utterance be found,
And magic hand touches the living core.
To you, across the cleft that time has torn,
(Not you nor I, nor any born today.
We are but pebbles that are washed away
Before the waking of another morn.)
I would in humbleness a tribute bring
To show I understand whereof you sing.

My heart was touched, my soul awoke in pain
As the dark moments of your life I felt
That, agonized, in your sad verses dwelt
And therein beat a somber, weird refrain.
Then suddenly, above this muffled beat,
Sweet as the trilling of a mated bird,
A gayer tune, a song of love I heard
As though you had been lured from your retreat
By dancing feet, by spring, by laughing eyes,
And had—casting your shroud of grief afar—
Flung pagan homage to some flashing star,
And worshipped Pan beneath the open skies.
Ah, you know how to twist the varied strands
Of life into your verse with magic hands!

September 12, 1951, was a great day for the 135th
Street Branch of the New York Public Library. It was

being renamed. This event was significant in many ways. The library had been expanded through the acquisition of the building directly behind it fronting on 136th Street. By coincidence this was the Madam Walker residence that had once housed The Dark Tower. The old building had been torn down and replaced with a new structure. Now there was a modernistic entrance marked in clear, bold letters, "Countee Cullen Branch, New York Public Library."

The people who had come here this Monday night listened to a program of simple dignity. Ralph Beals, director of the New York Public Library, presided. From the dozen Cullen poems that had been set to music, two had been chosen to establish the opening mood. They were "Tryst" and "If You Should Go." The melodious soprano voice of the soloist, Helen Phillips, of St. Louis, seemed just right for the delicate lyrics. Then the room was still as Ida Cullen rose to read. She began with "From the Dark Tower." Next she read "After a Visit," and she concluded on a light note with some selections from *The Lost Zoo.*

The man who spoke next had been chosen aptly. Charles S. Johnson, president of Fisk University, had been Countee's boss at *Opportunity* back in 1926.

"Countee Cullen was my friend," he began; then he modestly named the four people who, in his opinion, were highly placed in Cullen's esteem. They were Alain Locke, Langston Hughes, Arna Bontemps, and Harold Jackman. With clear insight he discussed the character of the young poet, referring specifically to his "unexcited eagerness for

202

the friendship of people and books." He spoke, too, of the Negro Renaissance, which he described as a period of both "sociological discovery" and "literary awakening." Of Cullen's place in this period Dr. Johnson said, "Countee Cullen was both a child and a midwife of this movement."

Then after Mrs. Homer, the branch librarian, had accepted from Mrs. Cullen the gift of her husband's papers and the soloist had finished the final Cullen songs, the audience came slowly back to the present. Many and varied memories had been revived by this ceremony. There were those who could remember a bright-eyed boy reaching to place his books on the circulation desk. Others thought of a teen-ager and his friends reading at their favorite library table. There were memories of a young teacher whose face lighted up with pleasure on seeing some of his junior high school boys voluntarily using the Harlem library. And the staff members recalled gratefully the many occasions when Countee Cullen had read to groups there, generously pouring his talents back into his own community.

There were some who had recently visited a simple grave in Woodlawn Cemetery. It was located on a rounded hill and marked by a rosebush. The granite stone was engraved: Cullen, Countee . . . 1903–1946 . . . Poet—Author—Scholar.

All of these people knew there would be disagreement concerning the status of Countee Cullen as a poet. But they also knew that as readers came across one of his poems in an anthology or held one of his books in their hands, they would be moved to act or to think. And many of these readers would conclude that the destiny of Countee Cullen had been to spread the gospel of beauty and justice in his modest, lyrical way.

Bibliography

Abrahams, Peter. *Tell Freedom*. New York: Alfred A. Knopf, 1954.

Bardolph, Richard. *The Negro Vanguard*. New York: Rinehart and Company, Inc., 1959.

Bontemps, Arna. "The Harlem Renaissance," *Saturday Review of Literature*. March 22, 1947.

Bullock, Ralph W. *In Spite of Handicaps*. New York: Association Press, 1927.

Butcher, Margaret Just. *The Negro in American Culture*. New York: Alfred A. Knopf, 1956.

Calverton, V. F. "The Negro's New Belligerent Attitude," *Current History*, September, 1929.

——. "The New Negro," *Current History*, February, 1926.

Cronyn, George. "Teaching by Scale," *The Modern School*, May, 1918.

Cullen, Countee. *Ballad of the Brown Girl*. New York: Harper and Brothers, 1927.

—— (ed.). *Caroling Dusk*. New York: Harper and Brothers, 1927.

——. *Color*. New York: Harper and Brothers, 1925.

——. *Copper Sun*. New York: Harper and Brothers, 1927.

——. *My Lives and How I Lost Them*. New York: Harper and Brothers, 1942.

——. *On These I Stand*. New York: Harper and Brothers, 1947.

——. *One Way to Heaven*. New York: Harper and Brothers, 1932.

——. *The Black Christ and Other Poems*. New York: Harper and Brothers, 1929.

——. *The Lost Zoo*. New York: Harper and Brothers, 1940.

——. *The Medea and Some Poems*. New York: Harper and Brothers, 1935.

Cullen, Frederick Asbury. *From Barefoot Town to Jerusalem*. (no publisher, no date).

Du Bois, William Edward Burghardt. "On Being Black," *The New Republic*, February 18, 1920.

———. "So the Girl Marries," *The Crisis*, June, 1928.

———. "The Dilemna of the Negro," *The American Mercury*, October, 1924.

Frazier, E. Franklin. "The American Negro's New Leaders," *Current History*, April, 1928.

Hare, Maud Cuney. *Negro Musicians and Their Music*. Washington, D.C.: The Associated Publishers, 1936.

Hill, Herbert (ed.). *Soon, One Morning*. New York: Alfred A. Knopf, 1963.

Hillyer, Robert. *In Pursuit of Poetry*. New York: McGraw-Hill Book Company, Inc., 1960.

Hughes, Langston. *The Big Sea*. New York: Alfred A. Knopf, 1940.

Hughes, Langston, and Bontemps, Arna. *The Poetry of the Negro 1746-1949*. Garden City: Doubleday and Company, Inc., 1949.

Johnson, James Weldon. *Black Manhattan*. New York: Alfred A. Knopf, 1930.

———. *The Book of American Negro Poetry*. New York: Harcourt, Brace and Company, 1931.

Locke, Alain (ed.). *The New Negro*. New York: Albert and Charles Boni, 1925.

Ottley, Roi. *'New World A-Coming'*. Boston: Houghton Mifflin Company, 1943.

Patterson, Haywood, and Conrad, Earl. *Scottsboro Boy*. Garden City: Doubleday and Company, Inc., 1950.

Redding, J. Saunders. *To Make a Poet Black*. The University of North Carolina Press, 1939.

Roosevelt, Eleanor. *If You Ask Me*. New York: D. Appleton-Century Company, Inc., 1946.

Thornhill, Gertrude C. "The Negro Becomes a Literary Contributor," *Poet Lore*, September, 1928.

Thurman, Wallace. "Negro Poets and Their Poetry," *Bookman*, July, 1928.

Untermyer, Louis. *Lives of the Poets*. New York: Simon and Schuster, 1959.

Van Vechten, Carl. "Ode to the Stage Door Canteen," *Theatre Arts*, April, 1943.

Wagner, Jean. *Les Poètes Nègres des États-Unis*. Paris: Librairie Istra, 1963.

Index